D1591004

Voice
for
Performance

Voice
for
Performance

Second Edition

Linda Gates

Limelight Editions
An Imprint of Hal Leonard Corporation

Limelight Editions
An Imprint of Hal Leonard Corporation
7777 West Bluemound Road
Milwaukee, WI 53213

Trade Book Division Editorial Offices
33 Plymouth Street, Suite 302, Montclair, NJ 07042

First edition published in 2000 by Applause Books

Second edition published in 2011 by Limelight Editions

Printed in the United States of America

Book design by Clare Cerullo

Library of Congress Cataloging-in-Publication Data

Gates, Linda.
  Voice for performance / by Linda Gates. -- 2nd ed.
      p. cm.
  ISBN 978-0-87910-353-8
  1. Acting. 2. Voice culture. I. Title.
  PN2071.S65G38 2009
  792.02'8--dc23
                        2008045119

www.limelighteditions.com

Contents

Acknowledgments

Thank You

The late Theodore Hoffman, one of the founding deans of the Tisch School of the Arts, who encouraged me as a voice teacher and gave me my first teaching job; George Hall, the former head of the Acting Course at the Central School of Speech and Drama in England, who convinced me that "the American musical was what was right with American theatre" and advised on the new chapter on singing; John Jones, Mary Corrigan, Cindy Gold, and Professor James Coakley for reading the manuscript and giving helpful constructive criticism; John Darling for his input on Chapter VIII and advice on recording the CD; Sam Ball for helping me scan the original text on to a disc; Sal Vito for his recording expertise, patient editing, and forbearance; my cousin, the late Martha Reynolds, for all the early editing and typing of the original manuscript; Linda Roethke, for undertaking the drawing of the illustrations at the very last minute; J. B. Capino for coming to my rescue in the computer labs when I was confounded by technology; Justin Bradshaw, for the computer chart; my colleagues at Northwestern, including Liz Luby, Alan Shefsky, and the late Claudia Kunin for technical support; Cathy Getch, for photographing my vocal cords; my students at Northwestern, whose hard work and enthusiasm continue to be an inspiration; my husband, George W. Tiller III, for his love, support, and endless patience; and my son, Christopher, who always believed I would finally do it.

Introduction

Perhaps no area of actor training is subject to more misunderstanding than that of voice and speech. Too often is it either cloaked in technical terminology that creates a barrier for the student to overcome, or there is controversy over which method or approach is the most effective. Today, even as many American actors are criticized for failing to measure up to the vocal skills of their British counterparts, voice and speech classes often do not receive a sufficiently prominent place in the curriculum of many American theater training programs. In some institutions voice is even *separated* from speech, as though the words of the language have no connection to the vocal instrument that produces them. What is worse, all this is taking place even as audiences and critics complain about their inability to hear or understand the actors on the stage. Then there is the growing spectacle of actors requiring microphones in the same theaters that a previous generation of actors were able to fill with ease.

The purpose of this book is to cut through some of the mystery and confusion surrounding voice and speech training for actors. While the focus is on the actor who wants to develop and strengthen his or her voice and speech for the professional theater, I hope it may interest and offer vocal guidance to the layman as well. Its aim is to develop a flexible vocal instrument that can convey the ideas, thoughts and feelings of the playwright in such a way that they can be easily heard and understood by an audience in the theater.

Included in the book are exercises developed over many years of teaching students of acting, both in the United States and in England. Eclectic in nature, it does not adhere to any one "system," but is influenced by the work of many fine teachers of theater voice and speech with whom it has been my privilege and great good fortune to work and to be influenced by. Among them are, Margaret Prendergast McLean, Edith Warman Skinner, Alice Hermes, Nora Dunfee, Kristin Linklater, Marjorie Phillips, Jane Cowell, Julia Wilson-Dixon, Cecily Berry, V. William Reed, John Jones, and George Hall and members of the Voice and Speech Trainers Association (VASTA), which continues to act as a support and resource through the years.

The format of this book has evolved out of requests by students for a book that would incorporate the work we do in class with an accompanying CD of the vocal exercises in the book, enabling them to practice with confidence on their own. While I firmly believe that it is important for a student to understand how the voice works and to have some knowledge of the mechanics involved, I have tried to keep the technical terminology to a minimum. This is not a book for the voice scientist; it is a book for actors.

Students of acting should realize that superb professional voices do not just happen; they are the result of both natural physical endowment as well as rigorous training, practice, and application. The goal of voice work is to reveal the heart and mind of the character through the words of the playwright so that audience can both hear and understand.

Chapter I
The Actor's Voice

When he speaks, the air, a charter'd libertine, is still.

Henry V *William Shakespeare*

When asked to describe those qualities they associate with a fine actor's voice, people will often use terms such as rich, resonant, powerful, commanding, strong, clear, easy to listen to, and so on. What gives the voice these qualities? Are they something with which the actor was born or are they acquired and developed through training?

The answer is that the actor's voice is developed in much the same way that one learns to play a musical instrument. While the quality of the instrument itself is important, it takes a great deal of study, practice, and application to master it and real talent to produce a superb artist. The human voice is, in fact, the most sublime musical instrument of them all; full of great range and subtlety, as with any musical instrument the first step in learning to play it is to find out how it works.

How the Voice Works

The primary function of the human vocal apparatus is surprisingly *not* the production of sound. Speech is a secondary function. Its first task is to enable us to eat, drink, and lift heavy objects. Its secondary task is to enable us to speak and sing. All serious study of the voice must take into consideration the primary function of the organs of speech, which helps us to understand what the voice can and cannot do.

The position of the larynx in primates indicates that early man probably could only communicate through a series of grunts and shrieks because the larynx was located high in the neck. As humans evolved, the vocal apparatus was modified lower in the neck, enabling the production of more articulate sound.

The sound of the voice originates in the larynx, a cartilaginous box located in the upper part of the trachea or windpipe. Inside the larynx are the vocal folds, or vocal cords as they are commonly known, which stretch across the inside of the trachea. The opening between the two vocal cords is known as the *glottis*. When we are not speaking or singing the vocal cords are open and relaxed, allowing air to pass through. There is a special flap called the *epiglottis* that prevents particles of food or water going through the open glottis into the lungs. If, as sometimes happens, water or particles of food start to enter the trachea through the glottis, we immediately begin to cough to prevent choking. The impulse to speak or sing immediately sends a signal to the brain which causes the vocal cords to adduct (come together). The pressure of the breath in the lungs causes the edges of the cords to vibrate. The speed of the vibration determines the pitch of the voice. The vocal cords also come together when we try to lift heavy objects. In fact, without the vocal cords, lifting would be very difficult and it is possible to become quite hoarse after a long period of heavy lifting.

It is not only the vibration of the vocal cords alone that produces the sound that we recognize as the human voice any more than a stretched violin string between two fixed points creates the sound we recognize as a violin. (Experiments on the dissected larynxes of cadavers show that when air is blown through the vocal cords it produces a sound much like the one a child makes when blowing through the lips to imitate a motor boat.) Once the vibration of the vocal cords is set in motion, the sound resonates through the mouth, pharynx (throat), sinus and nasal cavities of the head, and the chest cavity and is shaped by the lips, tongue, and movable jaw into the sounds that we recognize as human speech.

Of course knowledge of the anatomy and physiology of the voice will not in itself produce a fine voice because the vocal apparatus is controlled by involuntary muscles. We cannot will the vocal cords to come together, just as we cannot force the voice to produce a certain kind of sound. In fact, when the voice is properly supported and focused there is no sensation of the voice coming from the larynx at all. IF YOU FEEL YOUR VOICE IN THE LARYNX OR THROAT OR IF THERE IS ANY SENSE OF STRAIN OR DISCOMFORT AT ALL, THAT IS AN INDICATION THAT YOU ARE PROBABLY MISUSING YOUR VOICE.

Four Steps in Voice Production

The process of voice production can be summed up in four basic steps:

1. *Respiration*: the inhalation and controlled exhalation of the breath that vibrate the vocal cords.
2. *Vibration*: the coming together or adduction of the vocal cords to produce sound waves.
3. *Resonation*: the amplification of the sound waves in the mouth, pharynx (throat), sinus and nasal cavities of the head, and the chest cavity.
4. *Articulation*: the shaping of the sound waves into recognizable sounds.

Respiration

The first step in training the professional voice of the actor or singer is control of the breath.

When we are neither speaking nor singing the breath has a rhythm of its own. Inhalation and exhalation are a steady and regular motion—in and out. When we begin to speak or to sing however, the outgoing breath is controlled so that the pressure of the breath can vibrate the vocal cords. If too much air is released, the voice can sound harsh or strident because the speaker compensates for the lack of breath support by tensing the muscles in the neck and throat to "push" the voice out. This can result in vocal damage because the muscles in the throat and neck are also the muscles involved in voice production and can constrict the larynx, interfering with the smooth vibration of the vocal cords. Whenever you see an actor or singer red in the face with the cords in his neck standing out, the problem is inadequate control of the breath. For the professional voice user the intake of air must be rapid, silent, and invisible and the outgoing breath controlled and sustained.

Fundamentally the breath process goes something like this. When we breathe in, the air fills the lungs, which are made of expandable elastic tissue. The lungs are encased within the chest wall by a membrane (the *pleura*), which if punctured would cause the lungs to collapse. Within this membrane the lungs are subjected to a pressure *less* than that of the surrounding atmosphere. This means that the lungs are always somewhat inflated: even when we exhale completely, there is always some air left in them. As the lungs fill with air, they press downward on the diaphragm, a dome shaped muscle attached to the lower ribs. This causes the diaphragm to flatten and push the abdominal organs downward, creating more room in the chest cavity. When we exhale, the diaphragm resumes its dome shape as it is pressed upward by the abdominal organs to expel the air from the lungs.

The actor or singer must learn to control the outgoing breath so that a steady stream of pressurized air can vibrate the vocal cords. We will deal with this subject in detail in the chapter on breathing, but it is important to remember that control of the breath is the foundation on which all voice work must be based.

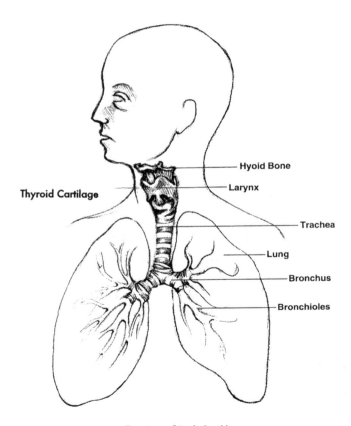

Courtesy of *Linda Roethke*

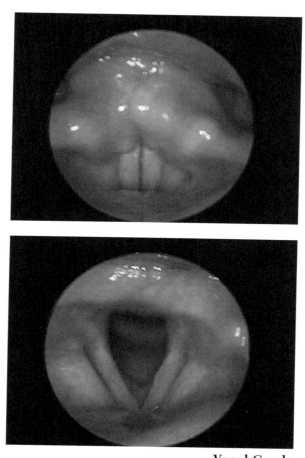

Vocal Cords

Courtesy of *Cathy Getch*

Vibration

The impulse to speak or to sing sends signals to the brain, setting up a complex series of adjustments in the larynx that cause the vocal cords to come together.

The larynx, commonly called the voice box, sits on top of cartilage rings that form the trachea or windpipe. Cartilage is an elastic material in the human body and makes up a large portion of the larynx. The thyroid cartilage ("Adam's Apple") is the most prominent part of the larynx. It is this part that you might see *protruding* from a person's neck. You can feel the thyroid cartilage if you tip your head back and put your fingers to your throat. Both the composition and the position of the thyroid cartilage are important because it acts as a shield for the delicate vocal apparatus inside. In fact, the word thyroid is derived from the Greek word for shield. Thus, the thyroid cartilage serves as the larynx's shield. The larynx is suspended by ligaments and muscles from a small U-shaped bone called the *hyoid bone*. Within the larynx, the vocal cords are attached at one end to the thyroid cartilage and at the other to the arytenoid cartilages, which are movable and allow the vocal cords to open for breathing and to come together for speaking and singing. In phonation the edges of the vocal cords are caused to vibrate at great speed as pressurized air from the lungs is sent through them.

The vocal cords can be likened to a reed instrument such as the organ or the oboe. One analogy compares them to the lips of a bugler. They are glistening white and constantly lubricated with a steady stream of mucous secreted by tiny glands located just above the vocal cords and in the nose. The mouth is lubricated mainly by saliva.

Male and Female Voice

Before puberty, there is almost no difference in size between the male and the female larynx. During puberty however, the male larynx almost doubles in size. The boy sopranos, whose vocal purity of tone is so valued in church choirs, lose their high notes as the vocal cords thicken. The female larynx, on the other hand, remains approximately the same size during puberty. There is usually the difference of an octave in pitch between the lower adult male voice and the female.

The length, thickness, and size of the vocal cords determine the pitch of the voice. The thicker and shorter the cords, the lower the pitch; the longer and thinner the cords the higher the pitch. Moreover, the cords may come together in segments to produce harmonics or overtones that give added beauty and color to the voice.

Although the vocal cords are under involuntary control, the voice student should understand something of their mechanism and maintain respect for the complicated apparatus on which so much of his or her career depends. One of the principal causes of most vocal problems is vocal abuse and many actors abuse their voices shamefully. As a professional voice coach I find that most of the problems I encounter when working with actors on a production are caused by vocal abuse or inappropriate demands on the voice.

I will be dealing with voice hygiene in detail in a later chapter, but if at this point any voice students are troubled with repeated hoarseness, frequent laryngitis, pain or discomfort in the throat or larynx, they should consult a competent laryngologist.

Resonation

Resonance is that quality in the voice which gives richness and timbre to the tone. It carries the actor's voice out over the theater enabling the audience to hear without strain. It is the hallmark of the professional voice.

Strike a tuning fork, hold it in the air, and then place it against a hollow object such as a guitar or an empty wooden box. The vibration of the tuning fork when held in the air becomes much stronger and richer when the tuning fork is placed against the guitar or box. The guitar is acting as a resonator which amplifies the sound.

The same process is at work in the human voice, only it is more subtle and complex. In essence the entire body acts as a resonator, the principal ones being the mouth, the throat and the sinus cavities of the head. The nasal cavity is also an important resonator and gives that special "ring" to the voice. The chest cavity gives added depth and richness to the lower pitches.

The resonators of the human voice differ from those of a musical instrument in that the main ones in the throat and mouth are movable, changing shape with each sound. In addition, they vary with each individual due to the infinite variations in the bone structure, size, and shape of the face and throat of each speaker. No two voices are alike any more than any two sets of fingerprints are alike.

Resonance can be felt as well as heard; it is a little like the sensation of humming. Remember, that this should not be felt directly in the larynx unless you were actually touching the larynx with your fingers. The voice should seem to be resonating in the *mask* or the frontal bones of the face.

We will be discussing resonance in greater detail (Chapter IV) with specific exercises to help develop it.

Articulation

Articulation is often rejected by voice students because they mistakenly associate it with "proper" or "refined" speech. Even today, despite the fact that the mumbling method actor has now become a caricature, many actors still fear that good speech will interfere with the naturalness and spontaneity of their acting. They are unaware that the process of shaping and articulating the sounds is part of the voice process and has nothing whatsoever to do with being refined.

The sounds of English are divided into vowels and consonants. Vowels are open sounds, which means that they can be sustained as long as the speaker or singer has breath. Consonants, on the other hand, are stops which divide the open vowels into syllables which make up words. Some consonants, because of their flowing melodic quality are even similar to vowels.

The action of the organs of articulation (the lips, the tongue, and the movable jaw), focus the voice forward in the "mask" or frontal bones of the face, placing the voice so it can resonate fully and be heard by an audience.

Effective articulation is extremely important for the actor because it determines whether he or she will be heard and understood without strain or vocal damage. It is also important for singers because the correct placement of the vowels and consonants improves the tone of the singing voice as well.

I hope that the beginning voice student will not become discouraged after reading this first chapter and say "but this is all too complicated, I can never remember all these things." Fortunately, with a well-trained voice the actor need only concentrate on the part he or she is playing, confident that the voice will respond. The establishment of a healthy, secure vocal technique means the actor doesn't have to think about the voice while performing.

Chapter II
Relaxation and Body Alignment

For this relief, much thanks.

Hamlet *William Shakespeare*

Tension is one of the hazards of modern life. It is something most of us have to cope with daily, and it takes its toll on our nerves, our health, and our emotional well-being. It is also one of the chief obstacles to good voice production.

The sources of tension are rooted in the pressure and stress of modern civilization. The daily assault on our nerves of noise, pollution, the fear of crime, and the anxiety caused by the pressure to succeed, financial insecurity, and concern for the future, as well as a host of other sources of stress cause us to "tense up" to meet the challenge. For the actor trying to make his or her way in a most insecure, demanding, and overcrowded profession, the effects can be especially devastating. The actor is particularly vulnerable because his tools are his body and his voice. If his body is rigid with tension, he will be incapable of expressing the physical and emotional life of his part with complete freedom. Since the voice reflects the entire well-being of the body, the voice from a tense body will be tense as well. It is therefore important that the first step in voice training for the actor should begin with the very real problems of tension. In order to combat tension it is necessary to understand what it is as well as some of its underlying causes.

What Is Tension?

Tension can be described as a reaction of the bodily systems through the muscles. In the human body there are two types of muscles: the *smooth* muscles, which control the inner mechanism of the body, such as the workings of the stomach, the liver, and the heart; and the *striped* muscles, which move the body's outer framework. The inner workings of the smooth muscles are involuntary—we can't control the digestion of our dinner any more than we can cause the vocal cords to come together by force of will. The striped muscles, on the other hand, are under direct conscious control and unlike the tireless, silent, and unobtrusive smooth muscles, they become stronger with exercise and weaken with disuse. Tension attacks both the smooth muscles and the striped muscles, manifesting itself in a variety of symptoms, both internal and external, such as high blood pressure, ulcers, heart disease, stroke, depression, headaches, insomnia, and an assortment of other ailments for which there is often not a clear medical diagnosis. Drug and alcohol abuse, cigarette smoking, and combinations of all three are symptoms of our desperate search for relief from tension.

Understanding some of the root causes of tension means that we must look to our past. To survive the perils of the primitive world they lived in, our early ancestors developed a physiological response when threatened called the "fight or flight syndrome." Danger or attack triggered an involuntary response that increased the blood pressure, causing the heart to beat faster; this in turn sent the blood rushing to the muscles, increasing the metabolism, and thus preparing them to stand and fight or to run away. Since natural selection rewarded those with the strongest responses, the "fight or flight syndrome" became ingrained in our physical makeup for which we still have reason to be grateful on occasion. A sudden movement in a dark room or a car that fails to heed a stop sign as we are crossing the street can set our pulse racing and leave us breathless when the danger, real or imagined, has passed.

Unfortunately, this response can also be triggered by the daily stress of modern life. For most of the circumstances we encounter every day, the choice of fighting or running away is not necessary; we find that we have "revved up our motor" only to have to turn it off again. In other words, the response that may have been very useful to someone fleeing a hungry lion will not be very useful to the actor preparing for an audition or facing an opening night.

Another source of tension is the rather sedentary lives most of us lead. Most experts agree that the best relief for tension is exercise; yet we ride in cars rather than walk, sit in soft chairs rather than hard straight ones, and in general pursue a lifestyle that allows our muscles to weaken with disuse. Once in a while we might decide to take up a sport or work out a bit, but usually we overdo it and give it up as soon as we find ourselves with sore aching muscles the next day. Again the problem is rooted in our early history.

When our early ancestors learned to stand erect rather than move around on all four limbs, it was quite an extraordinary achievement. In fact, man is the only animal that has managed it. His spine, which functioned very well in a horizontal position, now had to defy gravity and support the body as a vertical pillar. Since the chief function of the spine, apart from protecting the spinal cord and the nervous system, is the support of body weight and control of body movements, the additional pull of gravity meant that the muscular support system had to be stronger to keep man erect. Fortunately for man and his spine, the primitive world he lived in was tough and dangerous, requiring strenuous physical exertion to enable him to survive. He ran, he walked, he climbed up and down hills and valleys, over rough uneven ground; he sailed the oceans, crossed the deserts and frozen wastes, and he even challenged the supremacy of the birds in the air as he carved a civilization out of the wilderness. Having done all this he found that when he sat down to enjoy it all, his body rebelled. With no physical outlet for his nervous energy he developed tension, which uses up that energy without assisting the normal functioning of his system.

In order to combat tension we must begin to deal realistically with the needs of the body, both internally and externally, and to find a framework in which our bodies can function within the context of the stress of modern life. As we said earlier, the voice is a reflection of the body, not a separate entity in and of itself. Tension in the body will produce tension in the voice and no real improvement in vocal production can be realized unless the problem of tension is addressed.

Learning to Relax

The first step in learning to relax is to understand that relaxation is not the same thing as being inert, limp, or lethargic. Relaxation demands real muscular control and kinesthetic bodily awareness. This enables us to isolate and relax those muscles that are not involved in a specific physical activity so as not to interfere with those muscles that actually *perform* that activity. For example, in Act II, scene 3 of *Macbeth*, when the discovery of the murder of Duncan takes place, the actor playing Macduff must rouse the castle with the news.

Awake! Awake!
Ring the alarum-bell. Murder and treason!
Banquo and Donalbain! Malcolm awake!

It takes real muscular control to support and project the voice without vocal strain under the heightened emotional and physical demands of the part. If the cords in the actor's neck are standing out as he shouts, it indicates that he is tense because he is using the neck and shoulder muscles, which *interfere* with vocal production, rather than the diaphragmatic and intercostal muscles, which are responsible for vocal support.

Sometimes actors can be under a misconception about the terms "free" and "natural" as they apply to the voice. They believe that if they are completely relaxed then the voice will magically perform whatever is asked of it. Unfortunately this concept of relaxation is at variance with the actual working of the vocal mechanism, which is a complex muscular activity that requires the active participation of a complex set of muscles. Furthermore, they lose sight of the demands of the acting profession itself, which is hardly passive. An actor must not only be able to walk and talk at the same time, but sometimes, as *Cyrano de Bergerac*, fight a duel while speaking in rhymed couplets.

Ho, for a rime!...You are white as whey—
You break, you cower, you cringe, you crawl!
Tac! —and I parry your last essay:
So may the turn of a hand forestall
Life with its honey, death with its gall;
So may the turn of my fancy roam
Free, for a time, till the rimes recall,
Then, as I end the refrain, thrust home!
                Edmond Rostand

There are very few parts in the literature, except for death scenes, where the actor is prone. To be effective, our concept of relaxation should go beyond the vague notion of floating on a cloud to specific focus on the various muscular workings of the body and how to enable them to function in the most effective and productive way. In other words, we must move from the general to the specific when we deal with the problems of tension. The following exercises for relaxation and body alignment are some that I have found effective in my classes. They are easy to do and can easily be incorporated into your daily life. Be sure you read over each exercise carefully so you are familiar with the details and don't have to stop in the middle and refer back to the book. Repeat each exercise until you feel comfortable with it before you go on to the next one. Give yourself plenty of time and don't rush or you will defeat the whole purpose of the exercises, which is to induce relaxation, not tension.

Relaxation Exercises

Relaxation from Head to Toe

This exercise is to acquaint you with the sensation of relaxation by letting your imagination aid you in eliminating excess tension from your body. This can be performed as a separate exercise or as the first part of your warm-up. Be sure to allow enough *time* (at least 15 minutes) and find a quiet place where you can be alone and undisturbed. This exercise is also an excellent way to end the day and will help you relax and fall asleep.

- Pick a comfortable spot with a rug or a blanket to lie on and stretch out on the floor.
- Place your arms above your head and stretch them out while pointing your toes; *stretch, stretch*, now release and let go.
- Bring your arms down and place your hands on your middle just about on your bottom ribs. If you feel a slight arch in your lower back, bring your knees up, keeping your feet on the floor, contract lower back against the floor, then stretch out your legs again. Close your eyes, breathe in and out, feel the rise of your hands as you breathe in and the fall of your hands as you breathe out.
- Let your mind focus on your toes, feel them relax and let go. Be aware of the soles of your feet, the arch of your foot—let them relax and let go. Let your mind flow upwards to your ankles, your calves, your knees, thighs, buttocks, let them go; relax your abdomen, the muscles between your ribs and your chest; feel the rise and fall of your breath in and out under your hands; feel the

length of your spine on the floor, relax your shoulders and the back of your neck; relax your fingertips, the palms of your hands, feel the attachment between the hand and the wrist and let it go; relax your forearms, elbows, your upper arms, relax your throat, your jaw, your forehead, eyelids; mentally take each part of your body and feel the tension dissolve and relax. Feel the breath flowing easily in and out; imagine that your body is weightless and floating just above the floor. Take all the time you need with this exercise, don't hurry, just enjoy the feeling of your body at rest, at peace with itself, sustained by the rise and fall of the breath.

Now that you have experienced the sensation of relaxation while lying passively on the floor, let's begin to explore some of the principal causes of tension in our bodies when we are standing up. Obviously we can't spend our lives lying on the floor. Moreover, it's not a good idea to equate relaxation with lethargy because that can begin to short-circuit your energy, which is vital in acting.

Relaxation can be defined as a state in which there is no extraneous muscle activity beyond that required for the task at hand. If, as in the previous exercise, you are lying quietly on the floor, there is no need for any muscular activity other than inhalation and exhalation. On the other hand, if you are trying to lift a heavy table, it would be impossible without tensing the muscles in your arms, legs, and back. However, excess muscle tension, such as tightening the jaw, not only does not help you lift the table, but may interfere with the normal process of the vocal cords coming together, without which, lifting would be impossible. To begin to focus on tension in the body when we are standing up, we must first begin to understand the natural alignment of the body and its relation to tension and relaxation.

Relaxation and Body Alignment

Stand up straight! Pull your shoulders back! Chest out! Stomach in!! Don't slouch!!!

How many times have we heard these over the years? Is it any wonder that many of us slouched partly in self-defense? Unfortunately those well-meaning reminders may be partly responsible for our concave chests and curved spines as well as an enormous amount of physical inflexibility and tension. First of all, the body is not a straight inflexible pillar to be maintained upright at all costs. Instead, it is an intricate combination of parts whose precarious balance is always subject to the forces of gravity. Our goal is not ramrod straight military posture, but a flexible body in harmony and alignment with itself.

Exercises for Relaxation and Body Alignment

Basic Six Steps of Body Alignment

The following exercises, which I call the Basic Six Steps of Body Alignment. are designed to help you achieve good posture within the structural alignment of your own body. They are easy to do and should be practiced daily until their principles become second nature.

1. *Stand with your weight equally distributed on both feet.*
   If you begin by standing with your weight on both feet and then let the weight shift to your right foot, you will feel the right buttock tighten and throw the body slightly off balance. This causes unnecessary strain on the muscles at the base of the spine, causing you to lean forward slightly to relieve the pressure. Don't allow yourself to stand with your body weight focused on either your left or your right foot. Keep the weight equally distributed on both feet.
2. *Unlock your knees.*
   The knees are nature's shock absorbers. They cushion the body from the impact of the foot hitting the ground. If the knees are tightly locked, that impact will be felt right at the base of the spinal cord causing you to lean forward slightly to relieve the tension at the base of the spine. Tight knees also cause you to tip your pelvis back instead of forward.
3. *Tip your pelvis forward.*
   Place your hands on your pelvic bones and tip the pelvis forward from the base of the spine. This relieves the pressure at the base of the spine, relaxes the abdominal muscles, and keeps the lower torso in alignment. Just this simple expedient of keeping the pelvis forward will spare you possible back trouble in the future. If you seem to be having trouble tipping your pelvis forward, go to a wall, bend your knees, and contract the small of your back against the

wall, then slowly roll the spine up the wall while straightening your knees (don't lock them). Be aware of how the pelvis feels when you move away from the wall.

4. *Lift up the rib cage.*

    Think of the body as being in two sections—the lower torso and the upper torso, separated by the diaphragm, which is attached to the lower ribs. If you slump or slouch, the weight of the upper torso is dropped down, preventing the diaphragm from moving freely. This causes tension in the shoulder and neck muscles because they are attempting to compensate for the restricted diaphragm by lifting to help in the breathing process. A simple way to get the rib cage up is to bring your fingertips together and make a side upward circle until your hands are above your head. This automatically brings up the rib cage. Now bring your arms down, leaving your rib cage up.

5. *Let the shoulders drop.*

    Once you have completed the first four steps, simply relax your shoulders and let your arms hang at your sides, palms facing your thighs.

6. *Let your head sit on top of your spine.*

    You should feel that with this last step, your head is an extension of your spine. Don't pull your head up or push it out—just feel the spine lengthening out through the back of the head. If you are unsure if your head is in alignment with your spine, drop down and hang from the base of the spine, close your eyes, then slowly come up through the spine until your head comes up last and it feels as if it is sitting on the very top of the spine. Open your eyes. Your may feel as if your head is in a slightly different relationship to your spine, but it is now in alignment.

Exercise to Lengthen and Relax the Spine

Align the body using the Basic Six Steps of Body Alignment. Now imagine that there is a steel string threaded through each vertebra, beginning at the base of the spine, moving up through the small of the back, the middle of the back, through the shoulder blades, the back of the neck, and out through the top of the head. Imagine that someone is pulling that string and as a result the spine is being lengthened up, up, up toward the ceiling. There should be no tension in the legs, arms, neck, or shoulders, just the feeling of a gentle stretch through the spine. Release the imaginary steel string and let the head drop forward on the chest. Don't tense your shoulders, just let them drop and relax. Let your head roll to your right shoulder with the right ear parallel to the right shoulder. Feel the neck muscles stretch. Now let the head roll back allowing the jaw to drop open. Let the head roll from the back to the left shoulder, again keeping the left ear parallel to the left shoulder and feeling the stretch in the neck muscles. Now let the head roll forward and roll in circles to the right five times and then reverse the roll to the left five times. There should not be a pull on the spine, just the circular motion of the head rotating in a circle on top of the spine. Now let your head roll forward on to your chest again. Feel the weight of the head and your arms hanging easily at your sides. Keeping the knees unlocked, let the weight of your head slowly draw you down towards the floor. Do not pull or stretch downwards with your arms trying to reach the floor, just let them hang as the weight of your head brings you down. If your arms start to tense, shake them a little to make sure the muscles stay relaxed. With practice you should be able to drop down far enough so that your fingertips brush the floor, and as the muscles become more flexible, the knuckles and the back of the hands can rest on the floor. Now, just hang, easy and relaxed from the base of the spine. To come up, contract your abdominal muscles and let them bring you up slowly, vertebra by vertebra, until reaching the head.

Shoulder Lifts

Align the body using the Basic Six Steps of Body Alignment. Lift the right shoulder and let it drop. Lift the left shoulder and let it drop. Lift both shoulders and let them drop. Make a circle with the left shoulder, front to back, make a circle of the right shoulder front to back, make a circle of both shoulders together front to back. Now repeat the same shoulder circles back to front.

The Rag Doll Exercise

Stand with the weight on both feet and stretch your hands up to the ceiling. Reach for something just above you—reach right and reach left—stretch as high as you can, reaching with both hands, feeling the tension in your arms, neck and back. Release your right wrist and then your left wrist—let them go. Release your right elbow and then your left elbow—let them go. Release your right upper arm and then your left upper arm (your shoulders will still be tensed around your ears), now release your right shoulder and then your left shoulder, noticing the relief from tension as you let each part go and let your head float up on the base of the spine. Let your head drop forward on the chest and allow the weight of your head carry you straight down until you are hanging from the base of the spine with your hands brushing the floor. Begin at the base of the spine and come up vertebra-by-vertebra until your head is sitting on top of the spine.

The Relaxed Walk

An unexpected source of tension is the way we walk. If you observe a cross section of the population walking down the street, you will notice that most of them tend to lead with their heads. The second thing you will notice is that there is a slight jolt to the body as the foot hits the ground. With heads jutting forward from concave chests and curved spines, most people lumber through life instead of striding forth briskly. It is therefore hardly surprising that walking tends to be something that most people avoid whenever possible. Actually, the body is admirably designed for walking if we will only allow it to function as it was meant to.

Begin by aligning your body with the Basic Six Steps for Body Alignment that we have been practicing. Remember to always move from your *center* which is two or three inches above your navel and just below the sternum. If you lead with your head it will automatically draw your shoulders forward and collapse the chest. Instead, reach out with the heel of your foot, letting the weight of the body roll forward on to the ball of your foot. Let your arms relax and swing easily at your sides, with palms turned inward and your fingertips brushing your thighs. The bones of your feet are flexible and the weight of the body is meant to be shifted from the heel forward, across the balls of the feet and on to the toes which then push off, propelling the body forward as the body weight is then shifted to the other heel and the process repeats itself. Begin practicing in bare feet, but as soon as you feel comfortable with the new walk, switch to well-fitting shoes with a good heel. The toes turn out slightly as you walk and your knees should be relaxed and not locked, brushing each other slightly as you move.

Physical Warm-Up for Relaxation and Flexibility

The following exercises were worked out with Robin McFarquhar, a theater movement specialist. They are adapted from Hatha Yoga, as well as other systems, and are coordinated with the breathing. They should be attempted once the breathing work in the following chapter is established.

1. Sit on the floor with the legs crossed and the spine lengthened. Feel the length of the spine all the way up into the skull. Think of the back lengthening and widening. Inhale through your mouth and exhale through your nose; inhale through your nose and exhale through your mouth. Repeat five times. Take the time to do this slowly: it helps the body to relax and the mind to focus.
2. Contract the abdominal muscles with the spine curving outward as you exhale. Beginning at the base of the spine, lengthen up through the spine as you inhale. Repeat sequence eight times. Return to original sitting position with spine lengthened.
3. Lean forward, keeping the spine lengthened and straight right up through the skull. Inhale and exhale five times—return to center position. Turn upper torso to the right, lean forward, and repeat the inhalation and exhalation five times—return to center. Then turn upper torso to the left and repeat the inhalation and exhalation five times—return to center position.
4. Extend your arms to the side with the fingertips on the floor, keeping the back lengthened, and push yourself forward on your knees until you are positioned on your hands and knees. Inhale and exhale.
5. Contract spine down to the floor allowing the head to follow the spine upwards as you inhale. Contract abdominal muscles, arching the spine up as you exhale. Repeat five times.
6. Push forward with your hands placing the body in the "praying" position with your hands stretched out in front of you and your head on the floor. Inhale and exhale. Push forwards again to the hands and knees position.

7. Extend rib cage to the right and make a circle with the body, five times to the right. Then reverse the circle and extend the rib cage in a circle five times to the left. Inhale as the body arches upwards and exhale as the body moves downwards; reverse the process. Return to the "praying" position.

8. Keeping your palms on the floor, inhale as you push forward, following your nose until you have arched the body upwards. The head is arched back so that you can see the ceiling. Push back into the "praying" position as you exhale. Repeat four times. On the fifth stretch upwards, tuck your toes under you and push up, stretching the back of the legs. Then walk your feet toward your head (keeping the palms on the floor) and feel the spine lengthened. Then come up slowly vertebra-by-vertebra as you inhale. Stop when your hands are level with your knees.

9. Place your hands on your knees and contract the spine until it is flattened as you exhale—arch your spine upwards as you inhale. Repeat four times coning up through the spine on the fifth upwards arch as you inhale.

10. Reach up to the ceiling, stretch as far as you can. Then let the hands, elbows, shoulders, upper arms, head and upper torso drop as we did in the "Rag Doll Exercise" as you exhale.

11. Swing in a circle from the waist five times to the right and then five tiles to the left. Inhale as the body swings forward and exhale as the body swings forward again.

12. Hanging from the base of the spine, come up slowly, vertebra-by-vertebra, and come to a standing position with the body in alignment.

Relaxation of the Vocal Apparatus

The Soft Palate

The soft palate begins where the arch of the roof of the mouth becomes soft and ends in the *uvula*, a tag of flesh that hangs downwards into the throat. Tension in the soft palate can create a nasal twang or harsh metallic tone in the voice. The soft palate should be relaxed and flexible to allow it to lift or lower depending on the sounds being made.

The best exercise for the soft palate is a yawn. First, equip yourself with a mirror so you can see the soft palate and the throat. Firmly anchoring the tip of the tongue behind the lower front teeth, breathe in through your mouth and try to induce a yawn by lifting the soft palate as you breathe in. Don't worry, a yawn will come if you breathe in and lift the soft palate at the same time. Notice in your mirror that at the peak of the yawn, the uvula tips up into the pharynx creating a wide arch in the back of the mouth. Make sure throughout the yawn that the tip of the tongue stays behind the lower front teeth. With practice you should be able to induce a yawn at will and if you remember to simply anchor the tip of your tongue behind the lower front teeth when you yawn, every time you yawn you will give a good stretch to the soft palate. Incidentally, a flexible soft palate is primarily responsible for the "open throat" so prized by singers and actors alike.

The Tongue

The tongue is an organ vital to the production of human speech. It is also un-wieldy, and difficult to control. To get an idea of the shape of the human tongue, take a look at the beef tongues on display at the supermarket meat counter. You will see that the largest part of the tongue, *the root*, is at the back and that it ta-pers forward ending in a point at its *tip*. The human tongue has the same general shape, although it is, of course, smaller. It is attached at its root to the *hyoid bone*, a U-shaped bone to which the larynx is also attached. This close relationship between the larynx and the tongue make its relaxation and control vital to good voice production.

The tongue is actually two identical halves divided down the center at the midline. It is composed of a complex set of muscles that enable one section of the tongue to arch, narrow, or flatten while the other sections remain relaxed.

There are four sections to the tongue, beginning with the tip at the very front of the tongue; the blade, which is just behind the tip; and the middle and the back of the tongue, which is the part you feel against the soft palate when you say the "k" sound in the word "cake."

Take out a mirror, position yourself under good light and take a look at your tongue. First note the texture of the tongue itself. Is it deeply lined and creased, with deep indentations in the surface of the tongue? Is there a heavy coating on the tongue? If so, these may be indications of tension, vocal abuse, or nutritional deficiency. Now drop your jaw as if you were saying the vowel "ah." The tip of the tongue should be touching the back of the lower front teeth and the tongue should be able to lie flat in the floor of the mouth without bunching up or lying over the side molars. In some cases the alignment of the teeth or improper orthodontia may have left insufficient room for the tongue to lie flat in the mouth. (If your tongue cannot lie flat between the lower front teeth, you should consult a specialist to see what can be done.) Keeping the jaw in the dropped position of "ah," lift the tip of the tongue to the gum ridge, just behind the upper front teeth. Is there a pull under the tongue that prevents the tip of the tongue from touching the upper gum ridge without bringing the jaw up? If so you will have to do lots of tongue stretching exercises to stretch it. In extreme cases the membrane under the tongue (the frenum), may have to be surgically snipped to allow free movement of the tip of the tongue. (If that should be the case, don't panic; it is a very simple procedure and can easily be performed in the office of an oral surgeon).

Exercise for the Tip of the Tongue

As you watch in a mirror, touch the tip of your tongue to your finger tip. Touch very lightly and notice how it points. Be sure you are touching with the tip and not the blade, which is just behind the tip of the tongue. Now touch the tip of your tongue to the inside corners of the lips, first to the right and then to the left. Repeat until you can move your tongue smoothly and easily back and forth from corner to corner.

Exercise for the Root of the Tongue

Keeping the tip of the tongue behind the lower front teeth, drop your jaw and place both thumbs under your chin and swallow; the bulge you feel under your thumbs is the root of the tongue reacting to the act of swallowing. Now say "huh, huh, huh" as you feel the root of the tongue. If you feel a bulge under your thumbs when you produce the sound, this indicates that the root of the tongue is pushing to make that sound rather than being relaxed. Repeat the sounds "huh, huh, huh," until you are able to make the sound without pushing with the root of the tongue.

Exercise for Coordination of the Tip of the Tongue

Again using your mirror, place the tip of the tongue on the upper gum ridge. Notice that under the tongue is a V-shaped indentation with the point of the V ending at the tip of the tongue. The V-shaped indentation is formed by a pair of muscles that control the tip of the tongue and allow the sides of the tongue to spread and contract. The ability to control the tip of the tongue is vital to the production of the consonants **t, d, n, 1, ts, dz, s, z, sh, zh** and **th**. To strengthen the muscles that control the tip of the tongue, place the tip of the tongue on the gum ridge and softly intone the consonant **n** on an easy, comfortable pitch. Notice how the sides of the tongue spread for "**n**" which causes the sound to come through the nose (**n** is a nasal consonant) and the tongue should narrow slightly for "**L**" because the sound comes over the sides of the tongue. Now slowly intone first **n** and then **L**. If the V shape disappears that means that you are pushing with the back of the tongue, so stop, relax for a moment, take a breath and begin again. Repeat this exercise until the V shape in the underside of the tongue spreads and narrows easily and you are not pushing with the back of the tongue.

Exercise for Tongue Flexibility
Drop the jaw and let the tongue lie relaxed in the floor of the mouth. Keeping the jaw relaxed and down, bring the tip of the tongue up to the gum ridge and repeat "nah, nah, nah, lah, lah, lah." Begin slowly and don't let the jaw lift with the tip of the tongue. You may feel that the tongue is very awkward and that you don't have much control over it, but stick with it. If you absolutely cannot bring the tip of the tongue up for these sounds without tensing your jaw, you should have a dentist check to see whether the frenum under the tongue is too short.

The Lips
If the lips are tense they will not be able to shape sounds easily and freely. To relax the lips, blow through them in the same way a child does when imitating a motor boat or a car engine. Let the sound connect with the breath and let the voice move easily up and down the scale. It is impossible to strain your voice while doing this exercise: if the lips fail to vibrate, the sound stops.

Round the lips as though you were saying "oo" now spread them as in a smile. Repeat the rounding and smiling until you are able to do it quickly.

The Jaw
The importance of the jaw in good vocal production may come as a surprise, but

flexibility in the jaw is necessary for good tone production and articulation.

The lower jaw is movable and in some ways is rather delicate. It is attached to the skull just above the ear lobes by a small knob of bone called a *condyle*, which fits into a loose socket allowing the jaw to move freely up and down. It is also held in place by several ligaments that allow it to move in different directions as we chew or talk. If the jaw is rigidly held in place, it affects both vocal production and articulation as well, because the muscles that operate the larynx, the jaw, and the tongue are all interconnected.

Much concern is frequently expressed about a "tight jaw" and many exercises are prescribed for its relief. Tightness in the jaw, however, is a symptom rather than a cause of poor voice production. I have had many students come to me saying that tension in the jaw was their chief vocal problem and demonstrated exercises they had been practicing to loosen it. The problem was, that once they had finished their exercises and began to speak, their jaws were tense again. Most students find that once they establish good habits of vocal production, with special emphasis on articulation, they are no longer troubled by rigidity and tension in the jaw.

We must keep in mind that all parts of the vocal instrument are connected: poor posture, improper alignment of the teeth, inadequate control of the breath, lax articulation, and other problems all contribute to the voice as a whole. The jaw is not an isolated entity in and of itself.

Beginning voice students should develop a healthy respect for the jaw and not subject it to unnecessary abuse. Cracking ice or nuts with your teeth, yawning too widely or deeply, or even chewing a large wad of gum can strain the ligaments that control the jaw, causing pain or soreness around the condyle. Some people find that they grind their teeth when they sleep and this also can cause pain in the jaw area as well as damage to the teeth. If you are aware of a click or a grinding sensation as you move your jaw up and down, you should consult a dentist.

Exercise for Jaw Relaxation

Cup your hands under your jaw with your forefingers on the hinge or condyle just beside each ear. Gently let your jaw drop into your cupped hands and feel a yawn just under the soft palate, keeping your tongue behind your lower front teeth. Say the vowel "ah." Now take a breath and repeat "ha, ha, ha," keeping your jaw in your hands, easy and relaxed. Repeat this exercise on descending pitches. The jaw should not tense, rise or push in any way on these sounds.

Exercise for Flexibility of the Jaw

1. Say the sound "ma," letting the jaw drop for the "ah" sound. Now repeat "ma, ma, ma" allowing the jaw to move up for the "m" and down for the "ah."

   Repeat the exercise on the following sounds:

ba, ba, ba	ba, ba, ba	ba, ba, ba
ja, ja, ja	ja, ja, ja	ja, ja, ja
ba, ba, ya, ya	ba, ba, ya, ya	ba, ba, ya, ya

2. Round the lips for oo as in the word "who." Notice how the jaw drops forward and down. Now spread the lips for ee as in the word "ease." Notice how the jaw slides up and back. Practice going from one sound to the other.

oo—ee	oo—ee	oo—ee	oo—ee
ee—oo	ee—oo	ee—oo	ee—oo
aw—ee	aw—ee	aw—ee	aw—ee
ah—oo	ee—oo	ah—oo	ee—oo
ah—ee	aw—ee	ah—ee	aw—ee

3. Round the lips and let the jaw drop for the first two vowels, oo-aw, and then spread for ee.

oo-aw-ee	oo-aw-ee	oo-aw-ee	oo-aw-ee

   Repeat for oo-aw-ah-ee.

oo-aw-ah-ee	oo-aw-ah-ee	oo-aw-ah-ee	oo-aw-ah-ee

Summary

It has not been my intention in this chapter to cover every facet of relaxation. The exercises I have included are some of the same exercises that I use with my own students. I find they work very well in coordination with the voice and speech work. I would, however, strongly suggest that the serious student enroll in a class in body movement. Modern dance, fencing, Feldenkrais, Pilates, gymnastics, Yoga, martial arts, and T'ai Chi are excellent ways of developing a more flexible body. I would also suggest the Alexander Technique for further work in body alignment and relaxation. The main thing is to integrate movement and exercise into your daily lives and make a lifetime commitment to keep it there.

Chapter III
Breathing

How art thou out of breath when thou hast breath
To say to me that thou art out of breath

Romeo and Juliet *William Shakespeare*

When we consider how important control of the breath is to vocal production, it is surprising to discover how little time is devoted to making sure it is properly established. Perhaps this is because the subject seems, at first, to be a fairly simple and straightforward one and, as with relaxation and proper posture, breath control will take care of itself. For some students, this is the case; others continue to struggle with inadequate breath support throughout their careers. I have found that some actors, even those who have had singing training, will often have problems with control of the breath in speaking. One key factor is the lack of understanding of the specifics of the control of the breath and its relationship to the voice.

Recently, I worked with an actor whose speaking voice was pleasant but when she read from a dramatic text or performed an audition piece, it became a breathy, inaudible whisper. She gasped for breath after almost every other word and was completely out of breath at the end of each phrase. When I questioned her about what she was doing, she replied that she was releasing the breath to release the feeling. She was unaware that it was the pressure of the "unreleased" air in the lungs that vibrates the vocal cords and supports the tone. Unfortunately such misconceptions are not uncommon and can be very damaging to the voice as well as disconcerting to an audience when every phrase in punctuated with a release of breath. Efficient control of the breath is vital to good voice production and until it is automatic and secure, it will always be unreliable.

How Breath Control Works for the Voice

To understand how the process of breathing works for the voice is it necessary to know a little bit about the structure of the body.

The lungs are encased inside the bony "rib cage." As you can see from the drawing,

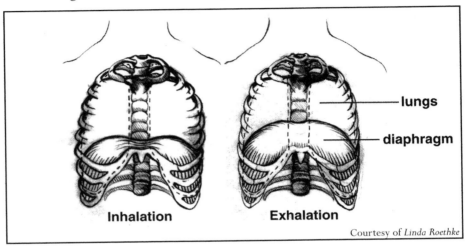

Courtesy of *Linda Roethke*

there are twelve ribs that radiate from the spine, forming an almost complete circle. The first seven ribs are joined at the front of the body by a bony plate called the *sternum*; the next three are joined to the ribs just above them, and the last two are unattached and are called floating ribs. Notice how the lower ribs arch up to the sternum, creating a space, which is unrestricted by bone, in the abdominal wall. This is known as the *epigastrium*. Between the ribs are sets of muscles called the *intercostals*, which stretch and enlarge the space between the ribs.

Attached to the lower ribs is the *diaphragm*, which arches up above the sternum. The diaphragm, as you may remember, is the sheet of muscle separating the upper torso (thorax) from the lower torso (abdomen). When we breathe in and the lungs fill with air, the diaphragm flattens downward, displacing the stomach, spleen, liver, and the other abdominal organs beneath it. When we exhale, the diaphragm resumes its dome shape. Sometimes you will hear a voice teacher say "place your hand on your diaphragm." Of course, this is literally impossible because in order to do that you would have to remove your head and place your hand inside your body. You can't actually "feel" your diaphragm, but what you can feel is the downward push of the diaphragm when you breathe in, by placing your hand on your epigastrium, which is the upper part of the abdominal wall just below the sternum. Of course, it does sound better to say "place your hand on your diaphragm" rather than "place your hand on your epigastrium," but at this point we will try to be accurate. What we are trying to establish is a place where we can feel the movement of the breath and get a sensory awareness of what is taking place as we breathe in and out.

Methods of Breathing

Chest Breathing

If you ask the average person to take a deep breath, exhale, and then inhale again, you will notice that most of them will lift their shoulders, pulling their chests up by the collar bones as they inhale, hold the breath, then exhale, dropping the chest and shoulders. If you are a beginning voice student then you probably do this too. This is called chest or *clavicular* breathing and it does have a function, although supporting the speaking or singing voice is not one of them.

Observe an exhausted athlete after a particular grueling game or a runner crossing the finish line. The athlete too lifts his or her shoulders and chest up and down because this method of breathing is the most efficient way to quickly replenish the body's oxygen supply. The human voice, however, needs a steady stream of *pressurized* air to vibrate the vocal cords and sustain the tone.

The problem with chest breathing for voice production is that when the shoulders and the chest are lifted, the breath can only be sustained by tensing the neck and shoulder muscles. This in turn creates tension that can interfere with the working of the larynx because the muscles of the neck and shoulders and the muscles that operate the larynx are too close not to be affected by the tension. Furthermore, because of the tension and strain caused by holding the chest and shoulders up, the tendency is to let them drop, thereby releasing the breath. It is at this point that vocal damage can occur. Deprived of an adequate supply of breath to support the voice, the neck and throat muscles try to compensate and may constrict the larynx as they attempt to sustain the tone without an adequate supply of breath. Sometimes you can actually see this when the cords on an actor or singer's neck stand out when they are performing. That is always a clear indication that there is inadequate control of the breath.

Diaphragmatic Breathing

Diaphragmatic breathing is the most commonly known method of breathing for the voice. With inhalation the diaphragm descends, displacing the abdominal organs beneath it. This can be felt through an expansion of the epigastrium just under the sternum.

Rib Breathing

This method of breathing is really an extension of diaphragmatic breathing, except the concentration is on the expansion of the ribs with the intake of air. Because the intercostal muscles between the ribs are very elastic, the expansion of the ribs provides for greater expansion of the lungs. A rather extreme version of rib breathing is called *rib reserve* whereby the ribs are forcibly held out at the sides, in front, and in back. This was popular at one time, mainly in England, but it is now felt to be too extreme because it produced unnecessary tension and strain. Another, now discredited, method of rib breathing is *pan-costal breathing*. This consisted of the chest and ribs being held very high, with the abdomen pulled in tightly underneath. This was based on the erroneous notion that the diaphragm arched up with inhalation rather than pushing down. This method was popular when whale bone corsets were the rage and has fortunately gone out with them.

Composite Breathing

The most efficient method of breathing is composite breathing. This is a combination of diaphragmatic and rib breathing. As the incoming breath lowers the diaphragm, it expands the ribs at the same time, providing extra room for the lungs to expand and muscular support to sustain the breath. It also seems to give extra richness and timbre to the lower tones of the voice.

Establishing Good Breath Control

The beginning voice student should remember that breathing for the voice is not just a technique to be employed on the stage when performing and then discarded when the curtain goes down. It must become a deeply ingrained personal habit if it is to be reliable. This means that a conscious effort must be made at the beginning to practice correctly, with consistency, and to incorporate that practice into your daily life.

Apart from being absolutely essential to good voice production, there are added benefits as far as health is concerned. Because you are breathing more deeply, your body gets added oxygen. Composite (or diaphragmatic-rib) breathing is especially beneficial to those who suffer from respiratory ailments such as asthma and emphysema because it allows inhalation without lifting the chest. Composite breathing is not difficult and can be mastered easily with daily practice. Consistent *daily* practice is the key.

Posture and Breathing

Good posture and body alignment are essential to good breathing habits for the voice. If you slouch or slump you will be dropping the weight of the upper torso on the lower torso which will inhibit the ability of the diaphragm to lower sufficiently for the breath. This will in turn encourage chest breathing because there will be no other way to get a sufficient amount of breath. Furthermore, if the pelvis is tipped back, rather than forward, the abdominal muscles will tighten, preventing their expansion as you breathe in. Be sure to you observe the Six Basic Steps of Body Alignment that we discussed in Chapter II as you practice your breathing exercises and incorporate them into your daily life.

Exercises for Breath Control

The easiest way to begin work on breathing is by lying down on the floor. By removing the pull of gravity, we can concentrate fully on the rise and fall of the breath without lifting the shoulders. It is also the way we used to breathe as babies and the way we breathe in deep sleep. Even the most confirmed chest breather will find it easier if they first begin on the floor.

Basic Floor Exercise
Take off your shoes and lie down on the floor. Stretch your arms above your head and stretch your legs downward, pointing your toes.

Stretch—stretch—stretch—relax. Repeat the stretching—pointing—re-laxing several times.

Now bend your knees upward with your feet flat on the floor. Contract your abdominal muscles, bringing your spine against the floor. Place your hands across your midsection, just under the sternum (the epigastrium, remember?). With your palms resting on the lower ribs, close your eyes and relax, breathing easily, in and out. Don't try to breathe too deeply or force the breath to expand the ribs, just feel the rise and fall of the breath under your hands. Be aware of how the incoming breath lifts your hands and how the outgoing breath lowers your hands. The chest and shoulders should be relaxed and still. Just remember—*when the breath comes in, the hands rise—when the breath goes out, the hands fall.* It sometimes helps to purse your lips as if you were sipping liquids when you inhale.

This exercise should be done for about ten minutes about five times a day. When you feel confident that you are thoroughly comfortable with it, place a heavy book under your hands and allow the breath to lift and lower the book. Re-member to let the *breath* do the lifting—don't just push the muscles in and out.

The Straw Exercise

Although this exercise can be done while lying on the floor, this should also be done standing, with the body aligned using the Basic Six Steps of Body Alignment.

Use an ordinary soda straw, the wider the better. Breathe in through the straw and out through the straw. Be aware of how the diaphragmatic muscles and the intercostals between the ribs expand with the breath and how the muscles handle the slow release of air through the straw.

Using a straw is an excellent method for those students who are having an especially difficult time with the shoulders lifting with the breath. You can use the straw to practice inhaling with all the breathing exercises.

Three Alternating Breathing Exercises

These three breathing exercises will help to increase the breath capacity, condi-tion the muscles involved in quick silent intake of air, and strengthen the muscles that sustain the outgoing breath. Once you understand how to do each of them separately, they should be practiced alternately to keep the muscles flexible.

Begin by concentrating on establishing your diaphragmatic breathing. Don't try to restrict the ribs, just let them expand with the breath naturally. Don't work for greater expansion of the ribs until your diaphragmatic breathing is secure.

These exercises can be done on the floor, but be sure to align the body in the Six Steps for Body Alignment when you do them standing up.

1. Blow out all the air in your lungs. Now slowly sip in air as if you were sipping through a straw. (The sipping is important because it keeps the throat from getting dry and it activates the diaphragmatic muscles.) Feel the diaphragmatic muscles and your ribs expand with the breath, making sure that the chest doesn't lift. After sipping in the air, hold the breath, then blow out. Repeat the exercise until you can do it easily and comfortably.

2. Blow out all the air in your lungs. Sip in the air as though you were sipping in through a straw in five little sips:

    One (sip), two (sip), three (sip), four (sip), five (sip)

Now hold the breath for a count of five—then release in five little puffs of air on a "pff" sound:

    One, (pff), two (pff) , three (pff), four (pff), five (pff)

Repeat this exercise, increasing the count to ten. Keep the rhythm easy and steady and don't overexpand.

3. Blow out all of the air in your lungs. Sip in air as though you were sipping through a straw. Now begin to pant lightly from your epigastrium or mid-center. Continue the pant as long as you can comfortably, then blow out the breath and repeat the exercise. You should practice this exercise until you can sustain the pant easily for at least twenty seconds. Eventually the pant should become a light, sustained quiver.

Exercise for Slow Exhalation

Blow out all the air in your lungs, sip in air, feeling the ribs expand with the breath. Release the breath very slowly on shhhh (until you feel that you are out of breath) then continue to release on the shhhh until you feel a slight "pull" in the diaphragm. Then release into the pull—breath will automatically come back in to the lungs. Repeat 5 times.

Begin to pant on sh-sh-sh-sh keeping a steady rhythm. Practice maintaining the pant and then catching a breath at regular intervals:

inhale   sh-sh-sh-sh-sh   (5 pants/catch breath/repeat)
inhale   sh-sh-sh-sh-sh sh-sh-sh (8 pants/catch breath/repeat)
inhale   sh-sh-sh-sh-sh-sh-sh-sh-sh-sh (10 pants/catch breath/repeat)

The intake of air should be quick and silent and the outgoing breath long and sustained.

You should finally be able to increase the number of pants before a breath and sustain the pant smoothly and easily for at least twenty seconds. Eventually the pant should become a light quiver.

Keep your focus on your breathing and practice these exercises until breathing with the diaphragmatic and intercostal muscles becomes second nature. Control of the breath is the foundation of all voice work.

Breathing and Speaking

The pressure of the breath in the lungs vibrates the vocal cords, creating sound. When the impulse to speak is transmitted from the brain to the vocal cords, they come together; when the voice stops, the vocal cords open. When you are speaking and pause for any reason, you should "catch" a breath, which means just replace the breath you have used. Let us say that you are on stage listening to another actor and must reply—the impulse to speak causes you to inhale before you begin to speak. Whenever you pause, no matter how short the pause, you should replace the amount of air you just used.

Example:

> *To be, or not to be; that is the question:*
> *Whether 'tis nobler in the mind to suffer*
> *The slings and arrows of outrageous fortune,*
> *Or to take arms against a sea of troubles,*
> *And, by opposing, end them.*
> *Hamlet* Shakespeare

The decision as to where to pause is up to the individual actor and the director; however, when he does pause, the actor should breathe. The following is an example of the possibilities for pauses and breath.

> *To be, or not to be (breath); that is the question (breath):*
> *Whether 'tis nobler in the mind to suffer*
> *The slings and arrows of outrageous fortune (breath),*
> *Or to take arms against a sea of troubles (breath),*
> *And, by opposing, end them. (breath).*

Exercises for a Catch Breath

A simple exercise is to count from one to twenty and upward, taking a breath after each *new* number.

> One (breath)
> One, two, (breath)
> One, two three, (breath)
> One, two, three, four, (breath)
> One, two, three, four, five, (breath), etc.

Continue to twenty and practice until you extend your capacity to thirty and beyond without strain. Make sure that you let one word run into the next until you come to the pause. Remember that when you pause, the vocal cords will open automatically and you will lose breath; moreover when you begin again, the vocal cords will come together quickly creating a glottal attack. It also helps to lift the last number before the breath in pitch on an upward inflection:

Example:

> One (breath)
> One-*two* (breath)
> One-two-*three* (breath)
> One-two-three-*four* (breath)
> One-two-three-four-*five* (breath)
> One-two-three-four-five-*six* (breath)
> One-two-three-four-five-six-*seven* (breath)

Summary

Avoid Overbreathing

A comfortable breath with a slight expansion in the rib cage and diaphragm lowered is much easier to control that a hyperextended breath that goes up into the chest. Remember that you will be replacing the breath that is supporting your speech at the next pause and not when you have used up all the breath in your lungs.

Don't "Sigh" Out a Breath Before You Speak

When you sigh on the first word in a line, you just sighed out your breath support! Be aware of your habitual speaking pattern to see if you are sighing before your speak.

Breathe Before You Speak

When you are speaking, even the smallest pause should be followed by a breath if the voice actually stops.

> "Ah!" (breath) "you don't say!"

Additional Practice Exercises

Take a quick catch breath between each line with the emphasis on telling the story. Don't rush.

> This is the house that Jack built.
>
> This is the malt that lay in the house that Jack built.
>
> This is the rat that ate the malt that lay in the house that Jack built.
>
> This is the cat that killed the rat that ate the malt that lay in the house that Jack built.
>
> This is the dog that worried the cat that killed the rat that ate the malt that lay in the house that Jack built.

This is the cow with the crumpled horn that tossed the dog that worried the cat that killed the rat that ate the malt that lay in the house that Jack built.

This is the maiden all forlorn that milked the cow with the crumpled horn that tossed the dog that worried the cat that killed the rat that ate the malt that lay in the house that Jack built.

This is the man all tattered and torn that kissed the maiden all forlorn that milked the cow with the crumpled horn that tossed the dog that worried the cat that killed the rat that ate the malt that lay in the house that Jack built.

This is the priest all shaven and shorn that married the man all tattered and torn that kissed the maiden all forlorn that milked the cow with the crumpled horn that tossed the dog that worried the cat that killed the rat that ate the malt that lay in the house that Jack built.

This is the cock that crowed in the morn that waked the priest all shaven and shorn that married the man all tattered and torn who kissed the maiden all forlorn that milked the cow with the crumpled horn that tossed the dog that worried the cat that killed the rat that ate the malt that lay in the house that Jack built.

This is the farmer sowing his corn that kept the cock that crowed in the morn that waked the priest all shaven and shorn that married the man all tattered and torn that kissed the maiden all forlorn that milked the cow with the crumpled horn that tossed the dog that worried the cat that killed the rat that ate the malt that lay in the house that Jack built.

This is the horse and the hound and the horn that belonged to the farmer sowing his corn that kept the cock that crowed in the morn that waked the priest all shaven and shorn that married the man all tattered and torn that kissed the maiden all forlorn that milked the cow with the crumpled horn that tossed the dog that worried the cat that killed the rat that ate the malt that lay in the house that Jack built.

Mother Goose

Chapter IV
Resonance

His voice was propertied
As all the tuned spheres, and that to friends;
But when he meant to quail and shake the orb
He was as rattling thunder.

Antony and Cleopatra *William Shakespeare*

Resonance is that quality in the voice that reinforces and amplifies the tone, giving it richness and power. It enables the actor to project his or her voice in a large space, allowing the audience to hear the voice without strain. It is the hallmark of the professional voice.

Resonance as defined in Webster's *New Universal Unabridged Dictionary* is "the reinforcement and prolongation of a sound by reflection or by vibration of other bodies," and in Cornelius L. Reid's *A Dictionary of Vocal Terminology*, "a spontaneous reinforcement and amplification of tonal vibrations which occurs whenever a cavity is tuned to the natural frequency of the pitch being sounded." In other words, a sound is amplified and made stronger by the sympathetic vibration of the body it resonates in. For example, a violin string stretched between two posts will not give off as much sound as the same string stretched across the body of a violin. The body of the violin acts as a resonator, amplifying and enriching the tone. Some violins, due to the unique combination of shape, age, varnish or other mysterious qualities, give off an extraordinary tone quality; while others, of the same shape and chemical analysis do not. The same phenomenon is true of the human voice. We will probably never discover the secret of the great actor or singer's voice in the laboratory or the dissecting room (although there are some scientists who are attempting to do just that). Great voices are mysterious acts of nature or gifts from God. We can, however, learn to develop greater resonance to enhance the qualities of the voice we were born with.

Vocal Resonance

Before we actually begin to work to develop resonance in our speaking voices, let us first examine vocal resonance to learn how it works. Resonance in the human voice is produced by the breath setting up vibrations of the vocal cords, which are then amplified by the resonators of the mouth, throat and pharynx, and possibly by the chest, the nasal cavity, and the sinuses as well. In fact, it can be said that in some respects the entire body acts as a resonator for the voice.

The chief way in which the resonators of the human voice differ from those of a musical instrument is that the main ones of the throat and mouth are movable, changing shape with each sound. In addition, they vary with each individual due to the infinite variation in the bone structure, size, and shape of the face and throat of each speaker. No two voices are alike, any more than any two sets of fingerprints are alike.

Resonance can be *felt* as well as heard—it is a little like the sensation of humming. Remember that this should not be felt directly in the larynx unless you were actually touching your throat with your fingers while you were making a sound. The voice should seem to be focused forward in the frontal bones of the face, often referred to as the *mask*.

Resonance and Pitch

The relationship of pitch to resonance in the human voice is subtle and complex. As we know, the human voice is capable of an infinite variety of tones, clicks, groans, grunts, and squeaks in an infinite variety of languages. The singing voice is especially capable of enormous range because it utilizes a change of registers as it moves from the "chest" voice" to the "head" voice. The chest voice denotes the lower part of the voice while the head voice or "falsetto" refers to the upper part of the range. It is, of course, possible to speak in a falsetto or a low growl if it is appropriate for certain parts, but they are not easily sustained. It is also difficult for the lower pitches to carry very well because the lower the pitch, the slower the vibration and the more difficult for the sound to carry and be understood by an audience. Higher pitches are easier to hear, but harder to understand due to the lack of vibration on the consonants. We will discuss this in more depth later on.

Optimal Pitch

Optimal pitch is the pitch or frequency at which the voice resonates with the greatest ease and clarity. It is determined by the unique vocal tract and physical structure of each individual. The first step in establishing good resonance in the speaking voice is to find the optimal pitch for each individual.

Finding Your Optimal Pitch

The easiest way to find your optimal pitch is to use the vibration of the *voiced* consonants, especially **m**. Say to yourself "uh hum-m-" feeling the voice resonate on the lips and through the nose. When you find the pitch that you feel gives you the richest sound, with the least effort, that will usually be your optimal pitch. This may vary from day-to-day, there is no one pitch such as a B flat that you can rely on day in and day out. The human voice reacts to changes in temperature, humidity, and climate and the notes may be slightly different from one day to the next. Your optimal pitch is an approximate group of notes that is right for each individual voice.

Obstacles to Using and Maintaining Optimal Pitch

When students begin to find their optimal pitch, using the voiced consonants as a guide, their first reaction is that the voice seems too high. There is a cultural bias toward a low voice, which is described as "sultry or sexy" in women and "deep and manly" in men. Many actors have consciously worked to push their pitches down. This results in a terrible toll in vocal abuse and can cause severe vocal damage. It is also not an accurate reflection of how the voice sounds to others. Because of the structure of the human auditory system, our ears, which lie flat against our head, only pick up reflected vibration of the sounds we make. Most of us are surprised to hear our voices on a taped recording and frequently think "that just doesn't sound like me!" This is because it is not really possible for us to hear ourselves accurately. When one is using optimum pitch, the same pitch which might at first, seem higher that the one we were used to using, is, in fact, perceived as lower by someone hearing it. This is due to the complexity of the vocal acoustic system, which I will try to explain as simply as possible.

The note which one speaks or sings is comprised not only of the note itself, but of other notes as well. If one holds down the low C on a piano while striking the C chord C-E-G in the treble a few times, very sharply, the low C will sound in the chord.

What all this means for the actor is that by finding and maintaining an optimal pitch, his or her voice will resonate with the full interplay of all the overtones it is capable of with the most efficiency and the least effort. On the other hand, using a pitch that is too low is hard on the vocal cords and does not carry well. Moreover, it will not have the color and richness which are contributed by the overtones. This is hard for some actors to accept, but it is vital if a flexible vocal instrument is to develop. Remember, that the ear is not necessarily the best guide for determining whether the pitch of the voice is the most effective when first beginning vocal training. In fact, the ear is usually the last to pick up on the accuracy of a sound. This is not surprising for if the ear had been able to hear whether the pitch was effective, it would have initiated that change in the first place.

Also, don't listen to yourself too closely as you speak. The voice should reflect the inner life of the character one is playing and the emotion that the character is expressing rather than listening for the correct tone placement.

Finally, the most important thing to remember about your voice is that if you "feel" your voice you are misusing it. The sensation of the voice, while it can of course be felt with the hand if you are touching your larynx, should be that of an open, empty throat. There should be no sensation of tension or strain in the throat when you are speaking or singing.

Resonance Exercises (follow on the CD)

Take an easy breath, allowing your diaphragmatic muscles and lower ribs to expand—feel the pressure of the breath sustained by these muscles. Now blow through your lips, feeling the vibration like a child imitating the sound of a motor boat. Let the sound end on m-m-m. Start the pitch as high as you can comfortably, letting the voice end on the pitch where m-m-m feels most comfortable.

Hum lightly on **m-m-m**. Feel the vibration on your lips and through your nose—move the sound down on fifths. Begin on an easy higher pitch—A above middle C is a good place to begin. Slide down the scale in fifths on **m-m-m** and drop the jaw, releasing the voice on "**ah.**" Work down through the scale in fifths letting the voice move from **M** to **ah.**

Using the three nasal consonants **m – n – ŋ**, intone on an easy middle pitch:

> **hum....ah**
> **hun.....ah**
> **hung....ah**

Intone "**hung,**" letting the **ng** sound come through the nose then slide into the vowels: **e...oh... aw... ah (iː oʊ, ɔː ɑː)**

Intone Vowels

> **ah....m....ah....n....ah....ng**
> **oh....m....oh....n....oh....ng**
> **aw....m....aw....n....aw....ng**
> **ee....m.....ee....n....ee.....ng**
> **oo....m.....oo....n....oo....ng**

Blow out, sip in, vocalize through lips on scale from top to bottom:

Intone: **m-m-m-m-m**
Intone: **m....ah.... m....ah.... m....ah**
Intone: **ba-ba-ba-ba-ba**
 la-ga-la-ga-la-ga
Intone: **me-may-my-mow-moo**
 lee-lay-lye-low-lou
 be-bay-by-bow-boo

Intone, keeping the pitch steady on one note at a time:

> **m-m-ah   m-m-ah**
> **hum-ah.....hun-ah.....hung-ah**

Keep the pitch steady and let the voice slide from one sound to the next. Chant on an easy middle pitch, moving the voice higher and lower:

The moan of doves in immemorial elms,
And the murmuring of innumerable bees.

Head Resonance and Chest Resonance

The performer's speaking voice is a balance between head resonance and chest resonance. When the voice is focused forward in the "mask" of the face, the chest resonator acts as a bass in much the same way as the bass of a stereo. Don't try to push the voice down for more chest resonance—keep the voice focused forward and let the chest resonate normally.

Exercises for the Head Resonator

Hum on the nasal consonant **m-m-m** then drop the jaw down to the vowel **"ah"** sustaining the **m-m-m** into **"ah."** Now using the forefinger up and down against the lips, intone the **"a"** sound. Notice the harmonic interplay of notes in the sounds. Repeat up and down the scale.

Exercise for Chest Resonance

1. Blow through your lips and on to the consonant **"m,"** dropping the jaw for the vowel **"ah"**; clasp the palms together and shake the upper torso. Sustain the vowel and let the chest resonate. Work up and down the scale through the middle and lower parts of the voice.
2. Place your hands on your chest. Inhale, then intone **"m-ah,"** focusing forward in the mask and at the same time feeling the vibration in the chest for the **"ah."** Repeat on lower pitches, blending the tone.

Connecting the Resonators

The speaking voice is a balance between the head resonators and the chest resonator. Lie on the floor with your knees raised. Place you hands across your midsection, breathe in, hold the breath and begin to pant. Keep the pant steady and don't push the muscle, let the breath do it.

> Pant on: **m-m-m-m** (feel the vibrations behind the upper lip)
> Pant on: **ha-ha-ha-ha** (feel the vibrations in the chest)

Move up and down in pitch feeling the resonance on the sounds as you pant. Remember the nasal consonants come through the nose; the vowels and other consonant sounds come through the mouth.

Once you have established the sustained sound lying down, repeat standing with the body aligned.

Finally, try to practice your resonance exercises daily until vocal resonance becomes secure and second nature. As we move into the next chapter on articulation of the sounds, remember that the voiced consonants should be the focus of resonance as well as the vowels.

Chapter V
The Sounds of English

Mend your speech a little,
Lest it may mar your fortune.

King Lear *William Shakespeare*

Somewhere at the dawn of man's earliest beginning, there occurred a great leap forward that set *homo sapiens* for all time above the other animals. Men and women adapted the mechanism of their larynx beyond its basic, physiological function of enabling them to avoid choking when eating and drinking, and began to communicate by using sounds. They then took another great stride forward and began to combine those sounds in such a way that they could be recognized and understood by other men and women. They created language.

At first it was only a spoken language, passed on orally from generation to generation. Then, as the civilization they were creating grew more complex, they began to search for ways to preserve and pass on their growing knowledge. Slowly, a written language evolved. Yet, at the heart of all written language is the spoken language, with its echoes of man's earliest attempts to communicate with sound.

The word for the closet relationship between the sound of a word and its meaning is *onomatopoeia*: cats purr, dogs growl or bark, pigs grunt or squeal, chicks peep, lions roar; fat sizzles, twigs snap, and waves crash on the shore, but it goes even deeper than that. Every school child knows that the best way to start a fight is to taunt another child with "nyah, nyah, nyah." The aggressiveness of the sound seems to provoke hostility. Another example is when a crowd gathers to watch a fireworks display, you can almost tell what is going on just by listening to the sounds the crowd makes: "OO-OO" when the rocket shoots up, "O-O-H" when it bursts into a shower of sparks, and an "A-H-H" as the sparks descend slowly to earth again.

These are the same sounds that you will find in the following words:

oo—plume, moon, doom, cool, ooze
oh—gold, snow, rose, glow, flow
ah—star, art, marvel, lark, harmony

The sounds of the words reflect the feeling that words convey on the written page.

Words and the sounds of words are for the actor what the notes of music are to the musician and what paint and canvas are to the painter. They are the means by which an actor expresses the ideas, thoughts, and feelings that are inherent in the written text that he or she must interpret. The actor should have full command of the sounds of his language. He should know how they are made, where they are placed in the mouth, and be able to get his tongue around them, to shape and articulate them. He should be able to connect his voice to the sounds and produce them clearly and audibly, without strain, so they can easily be heard and understood by an audience. In short, he must become a master of verbal communication.

The problems confronting the actor trying to master the sounds of words is inherent in the English language itself, which is one of the most unphonetic languages known to man. By "unphonetic," we mean that the language is rarely pronounced the way it is spelled. For instance, the words "boot" and "book" look as though they should be pronounced with the same long vowel, but they are not. The words "chute," "laugh," "cough," "guest," "debt," "phlegm," and "tough" are impossible to pronounce correctly just by looking at the words and sounding the letters. To add to the confusion, some words are pronounced alike but spelled differently and have different meanings, such as "do, dew, due" or "new, knew, gnu," "or, oar, ore," "I'll, isle, aisle," "two, to, too." Add to that the words which are spelled alike but have a different pronunciation and meaning such as "does" (verb), "does" (noun) or "bow" (verb), "bow" (noun), or "tear" (noun) and "tear" (verb). It is confusing, confounding, and irritating to anyone who sets out to learn the English language.

The following is an excerpt from a poem devised at NATO (North Atlantic Treaty Organization) to help its members smooth out their differing pronunciation and accents. A Frenchman is reported to have said in frustration that he would prefer six months hard labor to reading six lines of this aloud:

Dearest creature in Creation,
Study English pronunciation,
I will teach you in my verse:
Sounds like corpse, course, horse—and worse.
I will keep you, Suzy, busy,
Make your head with heat grow dizzy;
Tear in eye, your dress will tear
So shall I! Oh hear my prayer,
Just compare heart, beard, and heard,
Dies and diet, lord and word,
Sword, and sward, retain and Britain,
(Mind the latter, how it's written.)
Now I surely will not plague you,
With such words as vague and ague,
But be careful how you speak,
Say break, steak, but bleak, and streak;
Hear me say, devoid of trickery,
Daughter, laughter and Terpsichore,
Typhoid, measles, topsails, aisles,
Exiles, similes, and reviles;
....
Finally, which rhymes with enough,
Though, through, plough, cough or tough
Hiccough has the sound of cup,
My advice is—give it up!
          "The Chaos" Charivarius

The International Phonetic Alphabet

Fortunately, in 1886 a group of the greatest European linguistic scholars became so frustrated with the inadequacies of the Roman alphabet in the teaching of spoken languages that they banded together and formed The International Phonetic Association. By 1888, they had created The International Phonetic Alphabet, which gave a separate symbol to every sound in all the known languages.

Incidentally, one of those linguistic scholars was Henry Sweet of England, on whom George Bernard Shaw based the character of Henry Higgins in his play *Pygmalion*. The International Phonetic Alphabet (or IPA for short) is what we will be using in this book as we begin to study the sounds of the English language.

DON'T WORRY! The International Phonetic Alphabet is very easy and can be learned quite easily. Try to think of the phonetic symbols as musical notation and that the function of IPA is not to plague your life but to help you to acquire an aural sense of the sound much in the same way that a musician mentally pictures middle C when asked to play or write it.

We will be using the *printed* form of IPA, but try to practice writing the symbols by hand. Writing the symbols hastens the learning process. There is a close connection between the movement of the hand in writing and the act of speech. Children and even adults learning to write for the first time will unconsciously follow the movement of the pencil on the paper with their tongue as they shape the letters.

Prejudices About Speech Training

The beginning actor often comes to voice and speech training with a set of prejudices and questions that trouble him. Some of the following are typical:

• I've been doing just fine. Why should I have to change the way I speak?
• Won't my friends think I'm affected?
• I don't want to sound British!
• Will I still sound like me?
• Who decides the right way to pronounce a word?

Probably the best reason ever given for the necessity of training the actor's voice and speech was expressed by the great Russian director Constantine Stanislavski in his book *Building a Character*:

> It is absolutely necessary to be made aware of the deficiencies of your speech so that you can break yourself permanently of the habit, widespread among actors, of giving their own incorrect, everyday speech as an excuse for the slovenly ways of speaking on the stage. An actor should

know his own tongue in every particular. Of what use will all the subtle-ties of emotion be if they are expressed in poor speech.

An actor possessed of a fine vocal technique should *not* sound affected but rather be able to reveal the best part of himself through the character he is playing. If you are aware of the way an actor is speaking rather than what he is saying, he or she has not mastered the language skills required for his professional.

We will be learning *American* stage standard English. An actor should only sound British if he is playing a British character.

Finally, the rule for correct pronunciation of words is the same now as the one quoted by Horace 2,000 years ago: *"usus et jus et norma loguendi"* which means usage is the law or norm of speech. When in doubt consult a current dictionary.

The Sounds of English—Vowels, Diphthongs, Consonants

Vowels

Vowels are open sounds, produced by an uninterrupted flow of air vibrating the vocal cords. Vowel sounds can be long or short depending on the sound that follows or the stress of the syllables in a word.

You will notice in the Chart of the English Vowels that at the top of the chart there are three headings: *Front, Middle,* and *Back.* This refers to the position of the tongue. For the Front vowels the front of the tongue is arching forward, for the Middle vowels the middle of the tongue is arching forward, and for the Back vowels the back of the tongue is arching forward. For *all* vowel sounds the *tip* of the tongue is behind the lower front teeth.

This forward arching of the tongue allows the voice to flow up from the larynx past the large bulk of the root of the tongue into the resonators. Because of its unique muscular structure, the muscles in the tongue can work independently of each other. While the tip of the tongue remains behind the lower front teeth, the back of the tongue can articulate against the soft palate for the **k, g,** and **ŋ** consonants. This enables us to articulate quickly, as well as talk with our mouth full of food without choking.

There are three basic lip positions for all of the vowel sounds. The front vowels in American English take their shape from a slight natural *smile;* the middle

The English Vowel Chart

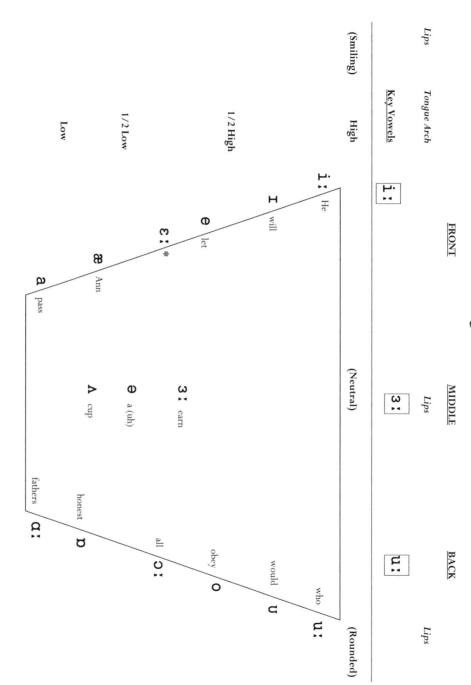

Lips | *Tongue Arch* | **Key Vowels** | High | 1/2 High | 1/2 Low | Low

(Smiling)

| FRONT | MIDDLE | BACK |

Lips | Lips | Lips

(Smiling) (Neutral) (Rounded)

iː   3ː   uː

iː He
ɪ will
e let
ɛː *
æ Ann
a pass

3ː earn
ə a (uh)
ʌ cup

uː who
ʊ would
o obey
ɔː all
ɒ honest

ɑː fathers

* **ɛː** is not pronounced as a pure vowel in standard English. It is only used as a diphthong (see page 67).

vowels from a *neutral* position; and the back vowels from a *rounded* position. These lip positions are important because they regulate the height of the jaw, which partly determines the size and shape of the mouth resonator.

Using the Vowel Chart

One of the chief difficulties in reproducing the correct pronunciation of individual sounds is to be certain that you are practicing the sound correctly when you are working alone without a teacher. Using the vowel chart in the following way will help you.

Key Vowels

The first front vowel **i:** (he), the first middle vowel **ɜ:** (earn) and the first back vowel **u:** (who) are your *key vowels* or the vowel whose initial position determines the shape of each succeeding vowel in that group. By taking the correct lip position for the key vowel, then dropping your jaw slightly for each succeeding vowel sound in that group, you will be able to make the correct sound. If your key vowel is right, then the ones that follow will be as well. It's a good idea to use a mirror to watch the position of the tongue and the shape of the lips and the jaw. Let's begin with the front vowels.

The Front Vowels

The front vowels in American English are formed from that most wonderful of all human expressions—a *smile*. (The emphasis on American English is that in British Standard English or "Received Pronunciation," the front vowels are derived from a *neutral* lip or *rounded* position although the arch of the front of the tongue is the same.)

Look into a mirror, think of something pleasant and smile. Notice that as you smile, the jaw is drawn up slightly and the inner shape of the mouth changes. Be careful not to let the smile become a grimace or a tight toothpaste ad—just an easy, relaxed smile will do. Now relax and let your face assume a neutral expression.

Again, with the tip of the tongue behind your lower front teeth, smile and say the first front vowel **i:** keeping the front of the tongue high and forward in the mouth. Now say "he." Repeat three times: "he, he, he."

Now let's go to the second front vowel **ɪ** as in "is." Begin with your key vowel **iː** say it, and then drop your jaw slightly for **ɪ**.

Remember **ɪ** is a short vowel and cannot be lengthened. Repeat three times: "it, it, it."

Go to the third front vowel **e**. Again, go back to your first key vowel, **iː** and say the sound, drop your jaw slightly for **ɪ**, then drop it again for **e**. Remember to retain the slight spread of the smile for the key vowel. Remember that the corners of the lips remain spread for all the front vowels. Repeat three times: "hem, hem, hem."

The fifth front vowel **æ** and the sixth front vowel **a** will sound almost alike to you as you begin practicing them. There is a slight difference though. The sixth front vowel **a** is one of the chief vowel differences between British R. P. and American Standard speech in words like "last, castle, dance, ask" and is also used in some British dialects in place of the fifth front vowel **æ**. Most American actors use the fifth front vowel exclusively, but be aware that the sixth front vowel **a** is sometimes asked for by a director wanting a "mid-Atlantic" sound, usually in classic plays because it is thought to have a more trans-Atlantic sound. The **a** is also used in the Irish, Scottish, and most northern British dialects.

Begin with your key vowel **iː** and let your jaw drop slightly for each succeeding vowel sound: **iː ɪ e æ**. Repeat three times: "ham, ham, ham."

The Middle Vowels

The middle vowels are formed from a neutral position of the lips—the jaw is half-low, the tip of the tongue is arching forward slightly.

The first middle vowel **ɜː** is the key vowel. It is not in itself difficult, but because it resembles the consonant **r** there is a tendency for the tongue to pull back. When you begin to say the vowel **ɜː** you may find that your tongue starts to arch back to make an **r**. It may take some practice to get it to stop pulling.

Begin with your key vowel **ɜː** and drop your jaw slightly for **ə**. Be sure to keep it very short: "her, her, her."

The second middle vowel **ə** is called a *schwa*. It is the weakest sound in the language and the one we probably use more than any other. It is always unstressed as in words such as "the," "a," "father," "above."

The third middle vowel **ʌ** is often called the "dull vowel" as it is found in words that have a heavy thud to them such as "glum, mud, gut, bump, ugly" but then again, it is prominent in words like "love, luck, up, and glove." Remember ʌ is short and should not be lengthened and is only used in a *stressed* syllable. Begin with your key vowel and work through the three middle vowels: **ɜː ə ʌ**

The Back Vowels

The back vowels begin with an extreme rounded position. To be sure you have the right shape for this sound, suck on the end of a pencil and then pull the pencil from your mouth. That should give you the right lip position. Notice when your lips are in this position that your jaw is automatically dropped slightly. Now with the tip of the tongue behind the lower front teeth and the back of the tongue arching high and forward, say the sound **uː** as in "who." Repeat three times "who, who, who."

Be sure to take a little breath before you make the sound. Use your mirror to make sure your lips remain in the same position through the sound. Now using your key vowel **uː** go through the back vowels in the same way we went through the front and the middle vowels.

The second back vowel **ʊ** as in the word "hood" is always short. Beginning with your key vowel **uː** say the sound, then drop the jaw slightly and repeat three times: "hood, hood, hood."

The third back vowel **o** is very short and should only be used in an unstressed syllable as in the word "obey" and "Ohio." Take the position for your key vowel **uː** then drop to **ʊ** and then to **o** Repeat three times: "Ohio, Ohio, Ohio."

The fourth back vowel then is a long, rich, resonant vowel. This is indicated by the two dots next to the letter. Going back to your key vowel **uː** then drop to **ʊ** then **o**, then **ɔː** "haul, haul, haul."

The fifth back vowel **ɒ** is very short and crisp. Sometimes the vowel **ɔː** or the vowel **ɑː** is substituted for it, but an actor should be able to say it easily. It is used in words like "honest" and "opportunity." Begin with your key vowel **uː** then drop to **ʊ** and then drop your jaw through **ɔː** until you get the fifth back vowel **ɒ** and repeat it three times: "honest, honest, honest."

The sixth back vowel **ɑː** is the most relaxed and open sound in the language. Begin with your key vowel **uː** then drop slowly through the back vowels until you get to **ɑː** as in "hark." Repeat three times "hark, hark, hark" keeping the tongue relaxed and down.

The Diphthongs

ĕĭ   ăĭ   ɔĭ   oŭ   aŭ

may   my   boy   go   now

Diphthongs are two vowel sounds which blend together to create one sound. They are made up of all the vowel sounds found in the Vowel Chart, as you can see from the Chart of the English Vowels and Dipthongs.

Most diphthongs can be long or short, depending on what follows them. This is indicated in phonetics by two dots, one after each sound. Above the second vowel is the little ˘ mark which is an unstressed mark to show that the second vowel is weaker than the first and is not given as much emphasis.

There are five short diphthongs in spoken English. They are called the diphthongs of R because they are used in words ending in R and always end in the schwa.

ɪɚ   ɛɚ   ʊɚ   ɔɚ   aɚ

peer   pair   poor   pour   par

The Triphongs

aɪɚ   aʊɚ

There are two triphongs in spoken English **aɪɚ** (fire) and **aɚ** (how). They are combinations of the diphthongs **aɪ** and **aʊ** followed by the schwa.

Vowel and Diphthong Length

The length of English vowels and diphthongs is not much of a problem for a native speaker of English because our ears are "tuned" to the sounds of the language. We don't have a problem with the length of the vowel sounds in words like "will," "with," "pull" or "take" and "vile"; we automatically know what the length of those vowels and diphthongs are because we are used to hearing them. For the foreign speaker it is a different story because short vowels and diphthongs may not exist in the native language. The result is that he or she will lengthen all vowel sounds, no matter what follows them and how they are used. Therefore, for the benefit of the actor who is not a native speaker of English, I am including all rules for the lengthening of both vowels and diphthongs. These will be shown in the Rules for Lengthening Vowels in the narrow transcription

The English Vowel and Diphthong Chart

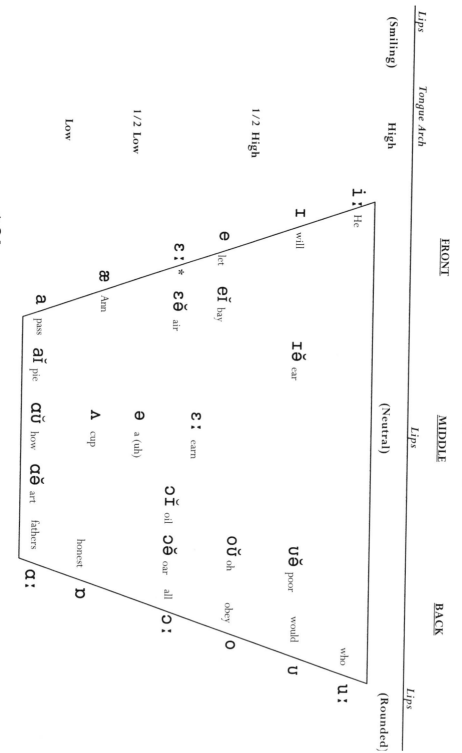

FRONT   MIDDLE   BACK

Lips (Smiling)   Lips (Neutral)   Lips (Rounded)

Tongue Arch

High

1/2 High

1/2 Low

Low

iː He

ɪ will

e let   ɛˑ *   eɪ̆ bay

ɪə̆ ear

ʊə̆ poor   would   who   uː

æ Ann   ɛɚ̆ air   ɛˑ earn   ɜˑ   oʊ̆ oh   obey   o   ʊ

a pass   aɪ̆ pie   ʌ cup   ə a (uh)   ɔɪ̆ oil   ɔə̆ oar   all   ɔˑ

aʊ̆ how   aə̆ art   fathers   honest   ɒ   ɑː

* ɛˑ is not pronounced as a pure vowel in standard English (it is only used a diphthong).

of the International Phonetic Alphabet, which indicates the difference in length through dots as in the following example using the vowel **iː** (me)

Fully long **iː**   (me)
Half long **iˑ**   (meat)
Short **i**   (meander)

Rules for Lengthening Vowels and Diphthongs

Vowels

The long vowels **iː, ɜː, uː, ɔː, ɑː,** are fully long:

- in a *stressed* syllable of a word before a pause:
  It's *me!* Who? He's *awful.* Be *calm.*
- in a *stressed* syllable of a word before a *voiced* consonant:
  meal, erred, wooed, awed, harm

The long vowels **iˑ, ɜˑ, uˑ, ɔˑ, ɑˑ** are half-long:

- in a syllable of a word before a *voiceless* consonant:
  grease, worse, boot, balk, heart

The long vowels **i, ɜ, u, ɔ, ɑ** may be short:

- in the unstressed syllable of a word: "meander, foresaw"
- in the weak form of "he, were, you, or, are"

The short vowels **ɪ, e, æ, ʌ, ʊ, ɒ** are always short. Lengthening distorts them.

Diphthongs

A diphthong is *long*: **eĭ, aĭ, ɔĭ, oŭ, aŭ**

- in a stressed syllable before a pause:
  "Hey! Hi. Boy! Oh? Ow!"
- in a stressed syllable before a voiced consonant:
  "pain, mine, toil, goal, brown"

Note: Exceptions to this are when one or more voiceless consonants follow the voiced consonant: "paint, pints, spoilt, colt, ousts"

A diphthong is *short*:
- in a stressed or unstressed syllable before a voiceless consonant:
  "fate, fight, oyster, oat, out"
- in the first syllable of words of two or more syllables:
  "fading, mating, playing, coiling, fighting"

The Diphthongs of R—ɪɚ, ɛɚ, ʊɚ, ɔɚ, ɑɚ—are always short and are never lengthened.

The English Consonants

A consonant is a speech sound in which the outgoing breath is stopped or impeded in some way. Consonants divide the open vowel sounds into syllables which form words.

A characteristic of consonants is that they may be *voiced* or *voiceless.* In a voiced consonant the vocal cords are in motion and the vibration can be felt by lightly touching the throat. Voiceless consonants, on the other hand, are produced by breath alone. Many consonants are identical except that one is voiced and one is voiceless as: sue-zoo, which-witch, toe-doe, fife-five, kay-gay, head-ahead, teeth-teethe.

Consonants and Pitch

One characteristic of the voiced consonants that is important for the actor to keep in mind is that when they are properly placed, they help to keep the voice focused forward in the *mask* of the face. This is because, unlike the vowels which have a very wide pitch range, consonants can be fully produced only from the middle of the vocal range. This is why singers often land lightly on the consonants when singing high notes. A soprano singing at the top of her register cannot sing the consonants clearly and shouldn't be expected to. In the speaking voice, however, the consonants reinforce the tone and focus the pitch.

The Chart of the English Consonants in
The International Phonetic Alphabet

Horizontal Rows indicate — *How the sounds are made*

Vertical Rows indicate — *Where they are made*

	Place I **Bi-Labial** Both Lips articulating against each other		Place II **Labio-dental** Lower lip articulating against upper front teeth		Place III **Dental** Tip of tongue on upper front teeth		Place IVa **Alveolar** Tip of tongue touching upper gum ridge just behind upper front teeth		Place IVb **Alveolar** Tip of tongue free and pointing towards **Front** of the gum ridge		Tip of tongue free and pointing towards **Middle** of the gum		Tip of tongue free and pointing towards **Back** of the gum ridge		Place V **Palatal** Front of the tongue articulating against the hard palate		Place VI **Velar** Back of the tongue articulating against the soft palate		Place VII **Glottal** In the larynx	
	VS	VD	VS	VD	VS	VD	VS	VD	VS	VD	VS	VD	VS	VD	VS	VD	VS	VD	VS	VD
Stop Plosives	p pea	b be					t to	d do									k key	g go		
Nasals		m me						n no										ŋ hang		
Lateral								l lay												
Fricatives			f fee	v vow	θ thigh	ð thy			s so	z zoo	ʃ shy	ʒ azure		r row					h he	
Glides	ʍ why	w we														j you				
Affricates							tʃ chew	dʒ joy												

Continuants

VS = voiceless / VD = voiced

Courtesy of Justin Bradshaw

The Consonant Chart

The best way to study the consonants is to use the consonant chart. This acts as a guide to show you how and where the consonants are made. Like the vowel chart, the consonant chart enables the student working alone to produce the sound correctly.

Look at the Consonant Chart; it can be read both horizontally and vertically. Reading the chart **horizontally** tells you *how* the consonants are made; reading it **vertically** tells you *where* they are made.

The English Consonant Chart

Stop-Plosives: **p-b   t-d   k-g**

Reading across the chart vertically, the first group of consonants are the stop-plosives **p-b t-d k-g**. The stop-plosives are aptly named as they are consonants in which the breath is stopped and then released. They can be *voiced* or *voiceless.*

In the voiceless stop-plosives **p t k** this release of breath is accompanied by a little puff of breath which is indicated in phonetics by a after the symbol ^{h} as in **hɒt^h**

Voiceless stop-plosives are released or aspirated before a pause, a vowel or diphthong.

Example: Stop!   tow   cow

When a voiceless stop-plosive is followed by another consonant, the consonant is held or unaspirated and not released, as in "mapped."

This is indicated in phonetics by a **p**₁ symbol after the sound. In the voiced stop-plosives **b d g** the voice is sharply released. One of the difficulties actors have with the voiced stop-plosives is in allowing the voice to stop before a voiced consonant is completed. Thus "Bob" becomes "Bop." Another is to let the voice drop back in the throat so that the final voiced stop-plosive becomes a grunt or a glottal stop.

In British English the voiceless stop-plosives followed by other consonants are released with more breath than in American English.

Continuants

Continuing down the chart, you will notice that the next three groups of consonants, the *Nasals, Laterals*, and *Fricatives* are enclosed in a bracket by the word *Continuants*. The Continuants are a group of consonants whose positions do not change as they are being made. The reason for this is that if the position of these consonants change while the sound is being made, the unstressed schwa is added, which gives the word a slightly pedantic and artificial sound.

> Example: "room uh." The additional consonant is called an *off-glide* and
> should be avoided.

Nasals

m   n   ŋ

The first group of continuants are the nasal consonants. These are the only sounds in English that are resonated through the nose. Nasal consonants are sometimes called semivowels because of they have the same properties as vowels for the actor or singer. The nasal consonants give richness and timbre to the tone of the voice and help give it focus.

Sometimes beginning students will avoid the nasal consonants in the mistaken idea that they will make the voice sound nasal. In fact, what they usually think of as nasality is just its opposite—*denasality*—a condition resembling and sounding like a perpetual head cold in which there is little, if any, nasal resonance whatsoever. (It should be pointed out, however, that any student suffering from chronic nasality or denasality that does not respond to any of the exercises in this book should consult a specialist to see if there is any organic reason for the condition).

Lateral

l

The second continuant is the consonant **l**, which is produced by the tip of the tongue touching the upper gum ridge, with the sound coming over the sides of the tongue. It is a lovely sound that is all too frequently allowed to drop back in the throat. It is also a semivowel.

The Fricatives

f-v   θ-ð   s-z   ʃ-ʒ   r   h

The fricatives are the third group of continuants. They are formed by the breath or voiced air being forced through an opening created by two parts of the speech apparatus coming together.

fie-vie   thigh-thy   sue-zoo   she-azure   row   head

The Glides

ʍ   w   j

The glides are accurately named because they begin in one position and then move quickly and smoothly into another. There are three glides in English. The first two, **ʍ w**, are pronounced the same way except that one is voiced and one is voiceless. Their initial position is the same as for the vowel **uː** as in "who."

Example: where-wear, which-witch, while-wile

The third glide, **j**, is only voiced and begins with the tip of the tongue in the position it would take for the first front vowel **iː** as in "he."

Example: year, you, cue

All the glides are semivowels.

The Affricates

tʃ   dʒ

The last group of the chart are the affricates **tʃ** and **dʒ**. These consist of two consonants blended together and pronounced as one. One is voiceless and the other is voiced.

Example: rich—ridge   batch—badge   catch—cage
           search—surge   fetch—fudge   latch—ledge

Articulating the Consonants

We are going to begin our work on articulation with the consonants. They provide a focus for the voice and help stabilize the pitch. They are grouped together, according to *The Manner of Articulation*, when the Consonant Chart is read horizontally.

The Nasal Consonants

m   n   ŋ

The English language has only three nasal sounds—**m n ŋ**. (In the French language there are nasal vowels, but these only concern us when we're speaking French or employing a French dialect for a play.)

We are going to begin with these three sounds because they are very resonant and it is easy to feel the vibrations at the points of articulation. What characterizes these three nasal consonants is that they are emitted through the nose.

m is made with both lips touching. There is a sense of vibration on the lips and in through the nose. Don't press the lips together too firmly or it will push the sound back in the throat—just let the sound vibrate on the lips and through the nose.

> **m   m   m**
> **m   (ah)   m**
> Mom, I'm home

n is made with the tip of the tongue against the gum ridge right behind the upper front teeth. The sides of the tongue spread slightly and the sound comes through the nose.

> **n   n   n**
> **n   (ah)   n**
> None are known

ŋ is made with the back of the tongue against the soft palate and the tip of the tongue against the lower front teeth. There are no words in English that begin with this sound—it occurs only in the middle or the end of a word.

> **ŋ   ŋ   ŋ**
> **ŋ   (ah)   ŋ**
> Bring our hangers.

Practice coordinating the three nasal consonants allowing the voice to come through the nose for the nasal consonants and the mouth for the vowel.

hum	ah	oh	oo	aw
hun	ah	oh	oo	aw
hung	ah	oh	oo	aw

Repeat on different pitches. Let the voice slide upwards in pitch on the nasal consonant.

m—ah   **n**—ah   **ŋ**—ah

Let the vowel sound slide into the nasal consonant.

ah—**m**	oo—**m**	oh—**m**
ah—**n**	oo—**n**	oh—**n**
ah—**ŋ**	oo—**ŋ**	oh—**ŋ**

Nasal Consonant Combinations

Practice the three nasal consonants with the fifth front vowel **ɑː**. Be careful not to nasalize the vowel.

hʌmɑː   hʌnɑː   hʌŋɑː

Initial

(No words in English begin with **ŋ**)

m

me	mix	maul
mill	make	mail
mull	moan	mire
may	my	more
mice	muss	mere

n

knee	no	now
nill	knot	next
nap	night	never
null	niece	new
nape	noble	near

Medial

m

human	common
framed	seems
demon	imp
plump	prompt
tempt	lump

n

alone	ground
final	tones
canal	opened
canned	groaned
sinner	pond

ŋ

rink	pink
angry	hunk
angle	zinc
stink	sphinx
lank	strength

Final

m		n		ŋ	
deem	rim	gone	drone	fang	bring
from	comb	ran	pain	clang	sing
came	frame	stain	gown	hung	thing
dream	roam	cane	fen	sting	strong

m	n	ŋ
bam	ban	bang
Sam	sand	sang
ham	hand	hang
ram	ran	rang
family	fancy	fang

Dan's fancy tankard   Sam's long entanglement
Francis' entangled Pamela   English Channel swimmer
damp lank hand   dangling Roman lantern
Long English Channel   managing strong kingdoms
damp, dank granary   fancy dangling lantern

Rules for the Use of ŋ

In some parts of the Northeast section of the United States, especially in New York, the consonant g is added incorrectly to the ŋ sound as in the words:

ri**ng**   si**ng**—si**ng**ing   Lo**ng** Island

Because English is not a strict phonetic language, pronunciation of these combinations can be confusing. Here are some basic rules.

1. Use only the ŋ sound at the end of a root word ending in "ng"

Example: sing, throng, strong, bring, prong, hang, clang

swing away	strong arms	searching an article
a gang of girls	hang a painting	thinking of you
singing along	reading a book	young singers

2. Use only the **ŋ** sound at the end of a root word with an added suffix:

> Example: hanger, singer, wringing, kingdom, clanging, bringer

singer of songs	longing for spring	bring a meringue
prolonging a song	hanging a painting	thronging crowd ·
cunning gangster	bringing a hanger	concerning drink

Exceptions: The superlative and comparative degrees of the adjectives *young*, *long*, *strong*, and *diphthongal, elongate, elongation, prolongate,* and *prolongation* have the **ŋ** plus **g** in the pronunciation.

a longer song	getting stronger	youngest son
longest dream	strongest arm	younger sister
slow elongation	he prolongates	it's diphthongal

3. Use the two consonants **ŋ** and **g** when 'ng' in the spelling occurs in the middle of a root word with no suffix:

> Example: finger, hunger, anger, English, strangle, linger

an angry manner	strangling jungle	a right angle
English linguist	extinguish the light	a cut finger
languishing lady	hungry angler	hungry enemy

Note: Exceptions to this rule occur in many proper nouns such as Binghamton, Arlington, and common nouns such as gingham and tungsten.

Selections for Practice

The moan of doves in immemorial elms,
And the murmuring of inumerable bees.
> *The Princess* Alfred, Lord Tennyson

No exorciser harm thee!
Nor no witchcraft charm thee!
Nothing ill come near thee!
Quiet consummation have;
And renownèd be thy grave.
> *Cymbeline* William Shakespeare

Moon on the field and the foam,
Moon on the mount and the wold,
Moon, bring him home! bring him home.
          The Cup Alfred, Lord Tennyson

And let me the canikin clink, clink;
And let me the canikin clink.
A soldier's a man;
A man's life's but a span;
Why then let a soldier drink.
          Othello William Shakespeare

Like a peal of broken bells—
Kling, klang, kling—
Far and high the wild geese cry
Spring! It is spring!
          Spring Celia Thaxter

"How many miles to Babylon?"
"Threescore miles and ten."
"Can I get there by candlelight?"
"Yes, and back again!
If your heels are nimble and light, You may get there by candlelight."
          Mother Goose

Ah, Moon of my Delight, that knows no wane,
The Moon of Heaven is rising once again.
How oft hereafter rising shall she look
Through this same Garden after me—in vain!
          The Rubiyat Of Omar Khayyam Edward Fitzgerald

They dined on Mince with slices of quince,
Which they ate with a runcible spoon,
And hand in hand on the edge of the sand,
They danced by the light of the moon

The moon! The moon!
They danced by the light of the moon!
     The Owl and the Pussycat Edward Lear

A drum, a drum, Macbeth doth come.
     Macbeth William Shakespeare

Hang out our banners on the outward walls.
The cry is still, "They come."
     Macbeth William Shakespeare

O what is that sound which so thrills the ear
Down in the valley, drumming, drumming?
Only the scarlet soldiers, dear,
The soldiers coming.
     O What Is That Sound W.H. Auden

Alone, alone, all, all alone,
Alone on a wide, wide, sea!
     The Rime of the Ancient Mariner Samuel Taylor Coleridge

Retreating and beating and meeting and sheeting,
Delaying and straying and playing and spraying,
Advancing and prancing and glancing and dancing,
Recoiling, turmoiling and toiling and boiling,
And gleaming and streaming and steaming and beaming.
     The Cataract of Lodore Robert Southey

There was a rustling that seemed like a bustling
Of merry crowds justling at pitching and hustling;
Small feet were pattering, wooden shoes clattering,
Little hands clapping, and little tongues chattering,
And like fowls in a barnyard when barley is scattering,
Out came the children running.
     The Pied Piper of Hamlin Robert Browning

The Stop-Plosive Consonants

p-b t-d k-g
The stop-plosives are consonants in which the breath is stopped and then released with a little puff of air. Stop-plosives can be *voiced* or *voiceless* and are made with both lips articulating together (Bi-Labial) **p-b** or the tip of the tongue against the upper gum ridge (alveolar) **t-d** or the back of the tongue against the soft palate (velar) **k-g**.

Both Lips

p-b
This voiceless stop-plosive **p** is made with both lips holding the breath and then releasing it with a little puff of air **pʰ pʰ pʰ**. You can actually feel the diaphragmatic muscles tense slightly as the breath is held for the stop and feel them release for the plosive.

Remember that this consonant is *aspirated* (released) before a *vowel* "paw," a *diphthong* "pie" or before a *pause* "Stop!"

It is *unaspirated* **pˡ** (unreleased) before another consonant, either in the same word or in the following word as in "stopped."

Practice Exercises:
Repeat **pʰ** several times. Feel the lips hold the breath for a few seconds on the stop before releasing the plosive. This helps to strengthen the muscles in the lips.

Initial
please	pea	plate	pit
palm	pay	picture	pop
pauper	pie	push	pack
poor	paw	pall	peer
peer	put	pool	purr

Medial

apply	apple	capped	supper
carpet	shipped	tipped	temper
suppose	rapture	opera	typing
open	capitol	zipper	frippery
superior	wiped	tempura	lapped

Final

hip	hop	fop	cop
drop	stop	drip	cap
clap	hope	cap	top
jump	heap	thump	trip
trap	rap	stripe	ripe

Practice the following words that begin and end with the aspirated p^h:

peep	poop	pip	pope
pep	pop	pap	pup
pipe	pauper	pooped	piped
pippen	peppery	pepper	Pippa
paper	popper	popular	pupa

Practice the following words with the unaspirated p^1:

apple	ripple	hips	cups
septic	stooped	paprika	ropes
apt	applaud	ripped	crippled
apply	stopped	scruples	conscripts
stoops	sprinkle	swept	corrupts

Selections for Practice

Speak the speech, I pray you, as I pronounced it to you,
Trippingly on the tongue; but if you mouth it as many of
our players do, I had as lief the town-crier spoke my lines.

  Hamlet William Shakespeare

Oh for a trap, a trap, a trap!
Just as he said this what should hap
At the chamber door but a gentle tap?
       The Pied Piper of Hamlin Robert Browning

Prithee Petruchio perchance your prattling prey is from Padua parted.
       The Taming of the Shrew William Shakespeare

And that government of the people, by the people and for the people, shall not
perish from the earth.
       The Gettysburg Address Abraham Lincoln

More happy love! more happy, happy love!
Forever warm and still to be enjoy'd
Forever panting, and forever young;
All breathing human passion far above,
That leaves a heart high-sorrowful and cloy'd
A burning forehead, and a parching tongue.
       Ode on a Grecian Urn John Keats

b

The voiced stop-plosive **b** is made with both lips coming together and releasing
the sound. There is a sensation of vibrations on the lips. Don't drop the jaw or
you will be adding the schwa which is called an *off-glide*.

    Example: rob   rob (uh)

Practice Exercises

    b b b b
    b b b   bob—bob—bob
    bob—bob—bob—bob
    be—buy—bay—bow—boo

Initial

bat	bean	boot	boil
bucolic	bib	book	bone
bark	bed	bought	bower
burr	babble	balk	beer
bog	blanche	balm	bare

Medial

fibber	ribbed	crumble	Mabel
robber	dubious	stable	robed
vibrate	dabble	hobby	disburse
symbol	amble	crabs	cabbage
crumble	harbor	cable	robin

Final

crab	swab	sob	gab
tribe	club	drub	fob
cub	boob	cob	nab
robe	mob	lob	bribe
stab	dub	tub	tube

Consonant Combinations

reap benefits	pop balloons
scrap book	top banana
ripe plums	probably broken
stripped ribbon	peppery papaya
brown paper	robbery suspect
club basement	curb battle
rob banks	rib break
stop payment	top position
keep promises	rip pattern

Selections for Practice

Whereat, with blade, with bloody blameful blade
He bravely broach'd his boiling bloody breast.
> *A Midsummer Night's Dream* William Shakespeare

A bow shot from her bower eaves,
He rode between the barley-sheaves,
The sun came dazzling thro' the leaves,
And flamed upon the brazen greaves
Of bold Sir Lancelot.
> *The Lady of Shalott* Alfred, Lord Tennyson

Beat an empty barrel with the handle of a broom,
Boom, boom, boom!
> *The Congo* Vachel Lindsay

Beaten, badly beaten, Hal; Ah but bawdy banter and sack
Soon will banish our blue-lived humor.
> *Henry IV, Part 1* William Shakespeare

Double, double, toil and trouble;
Fire burn and cauldron bubble.
> *Macbeth* William Shakespeare

All the breath and the bloom of the year in the bag of one bee.
> Robert Browning

So, buy of your Buttercup, dear little Buttercup
Sailors should never be shy;
So, buy of your Buttercup—poor little Buttercup;
Come of your Buttercup buy!
> *H.M.S. Pinafore* W. S. Gilbert

Bloody the billows were boiling there
Turbid the tide of tumbling waves
Horribly seething with sword blood hot.
> *Beowulf* Gummere Translation

Trumpets are sounding,
War-steeds are bounding,
Stand to your arms, and march in good order,
England shall many a day
Tell of the bloody fray,
When the Blue Bonnets came over the Border.
> *The Monastery* Sir Walter Scott

Behold, the bush burned with fire, and the bush was not consumed.
> *Exodus 2:3*

Tip of the Tongue

t-d

The stop-plosives **t-d** are made with the tip of the tongue articulating against the upper gum ridge. Make sure you are using the tip of the tongue and not the *blade*, which is the part of the tongue right behind the tip, otherwise the sound will be thick and slightly muffled. In the voiceless stop-plosive **t** the tip of the tongue holds the breath and then releases it with a little puff. The tip of the tongue does not drop behind the lower front teeth after the puff, but remains just off the gum ridge until the sound is completed. Don't tighten the jaw—the tip of the tongue does it all.

Place the tip of the tongue on the gum ridge. Release the breath firmly with the tip of the tongue: **t-t-t-t-t   t-t-t-t-t   t-t-t-t-t**

tah, tuh	tah, tuh	tah, tuh
toot tuh	toot tuh	toot tuh
tee tay	tee tay	tee tay
toy toy	toy toy	toy toy
tah tee	tah tee	tah tee

Initial

teat	toot	tattle	Tate
tit	tootsie	tight	time
tet	tote	tot	trendy
tat	taut	tout	twenty
teak	teal	town	touch

Note: **t** is *unaspirated* **t**₁ (unreleased) before another consonant, either in the same word or in the following word as in "bitten." **t₁n**

little	mostly	cotton	shirstwaist	costly
mitten	cattle	Brighton	battle	bottle

Medial

fattest kitty	better butter	lighter batter
whiter shutter	cute sitter	pitter patter
mighty putter	bitter voter	a lot smarter
tighter sweater	later letter	better lighter
little mites	fitter fettle	brittle chatter

Final

nipped	bit wet	caught sight
hot tarte	tight shirtwaist	ate meat
first date	smart vote	at night
right start	worst tale	right time
worst flight	night court	slight smart

Consonant Combinations

toot at Tut	bright star	tired teetotaler
tea for two	team tug	times ten
Tom's team	twenty-two	ten tanks
sweet tart	tight shirtwaist	late seat
list serve	mast torn	night time

Selections for Practice

Teasing Tom was a very bad boy;
A great big squirt was his favorite toy;

He put live shrimps in his father's boots,
And sewed up the sleeves of his Sunday suits;
He punched his poor little sisters' heads,
And cayenne-peppered their four-post beds;
He plastered their hair with cobbler's wax,
And dropped hot half pennies down their backs.
      Patience W. S. Gilbert

Don't you love to lie and listen
Listen to the rain,
With its little patter, patter
And its tiny clatter, clatter
And its silvery spatter, spatter
On the roof and on the pane.
      Clinton Scallard

'T'is fit the forest fall,
The steep be graded,
The mountain tunneled,
The sand shaded
The orchard planted,
The glebe tilled,
The prairie granted,
The steamer built.
      Ode Ralph Waldo Emerson

The Devil, having nothing else to do,
Went off to tempt My Lady Poltagrue.
My Lady, tempted by a private whim,
To his extreme annoyance, tempted him.
      On Lady Poltagrue, A Public Peril Hilaire Belloc

What a tale of terror, now, their turbulency tells:
In the startled ear of night
How they scream out their affright!

Too much horrified to speak,
They can only shriek, shriek,
Out of tune.
> *The Bells* Edgar Allen Poe

d
The voiced stop-plosive **d** is made on the gum ridge behind the upper front teeth.

Initial

deed	dude	drowned	Dade
did	dodo	dwindle	died
dead	Dodd	dwarf	Dowd
dad	Dada	doth	dared
deal	disk	did'st	dip

Medial

wider	ladder	paded	cradle
widow	faddest	needled	fiendish
murder	hardest	deeded	riding
reddest	candy	garden	larder
ruder	bobbin	beamed	brindled

Final

rude	jade	dread	gloved
waved	mouthed	tithed	loathed
leaned	command	wound	pined
eased	field	bald	rigged
bulged	baffled	leveled	waddled

Final "ed" Endings
When a word ends in "ed," if the preceeding consonant is voiceless it is pronounced with a "**t**." If it is voiced it is pronounced with a "**d**."

p, t		b d	
ripped	whipped	stabbed	robed
nipped	shipped	ribbed	fibbed

capped	topped	bribed	clubbed
hoped	stopped	curbed	jobbed
taped	flopped	flubbed	bobbed

Consonant Combinations

booed Fred	red bird	bold maid
dead weed	added word	cold wind
kind deed	fried bread	wounded bird
unweeded garden	borrowed gold	bad kid
bordered wood	weird friend	sound order

Selections for Practice

There was an old man with a beard,
Who said, It is just as I feared,—
Two owls and a hen,
Four larks and a wren
Have all built their nests in my beard.

    Edward Lear

Think you a little din can daunt mine ears?

    The Taming of the Shrew William Shakespeare

When to evade Destruction's hand,
To hide they all proceeded
No soldier in that gallant band
Hid half as well as he did.

    The Gondoliers W. S. Gilbert

If every ducat in six thousand ducats
Were in six parts and every part a ducat,
I would not draw them; I would have my bond.

    The Merchant of Venice William Shakespeare

Why she's a devil, a devil, the devil's dam.

    The Taming of the Shrew William Shakespeare

Rivers and Dorset, you were standers by,—
And so wast thou, Lord Hastings,—when my son
Was stabb'd with bloody daggers:
>   *Richard III* William Shakespeare

Come when you're called,
Do what you're bid,
Shut the door after you,
And never be chid.
>   *Mother Goose*

This I beheld, or dreamed it in a dream;
There spread a cloud of dust along a plain;
And underneath the cloud, or in it, raged
A furious battle, and men yelled, and swords
Shocked upon swords and shields.
>   *Opportunity* Edward Rowland Sill

When the lamp is shattered
The light in the dust lies dead—
When the cloud is scattered
The rainbow's glory is shed.
>   *When the Lamp is Shattered* Percy Bysshe Shelley

What dreadful dole is here?
Eyes do you see?
How can it be?
O Dainty duck! O dear!
>   *A Midsummer Night's Dream* William Shakespeare

Back of the Tongue

k-g

The stop-plosives **k-g** are made with the back of the tongue against the soft palate. The tip of the tongue is relaxed and remains behind the lower front teeth.

The position is the same for both sounds only **k** is voiceless and **g** is voiced.

k

Initial

key	cook	calm	kier
kin	could	cur	care
Celt	co-op	cup	Coors
cat	caul	Kate	core
cask	caucus	coward	kale

Medial

rebuked	shrieked	exact	kicked
worked	licked	ached	vehicle
ducks	conduct	locked	slaked
sex	ax	flakes	creeks
squint	scheme	scuffle	skein

Final

beak	fluke	ilk	thank
pick	duke	silk	sink
eke	brook	elk	drink
peck	walk	bulk	dank
pack	lock	hulk	drunk

Consonant Combinations

kick boxing	fake character	rebukes Ike
actual conflict	lucky instincts	knickerty knock
rejected recruit	cankered cutting	crawling crabs

Selections for Practice

By the pricking of my thumbs
Something wicked this way comes.
Open locks, whoever knocks!

Macbeth William Shakespeare

You lie, in faith; for you are call'd plain Kate,
And bonny Kate, and sometimes Kate the curst;
But, Kate the prettiest Kate in Christendom;
Kate of Kate-Hall, my super-dainty Kate,
For dainties are all Kates; and therefore, Kate,
Take this of me, Kate of my consolation;
Hearing thy mildness prais'd in every town,
Thy virtues spoke of, and thy beauty sounded—
Yet not so deeply as to thee belongs—
Myself am mov'd to woo thee for my wife.
   The Taming of the Shrew William Shakespeare

Not, I'll not, carrion comfort, Despair, not feast on thee;
Not untwist—slack they may be—these last strands of man
In me ór, most weary, cry *I can no more*. I can;
Can something, hope, wish day come, not choose not to be.
   Carrion Comfort Gerard Manley Hopkins

She was nervous, cataleptic,
And anemic and dyspeptic
Though not convinced of apoplexy, yet she had her fears.
She dwelt with force fanatical,
Upon a twinge rheumatical,
And said she had a buzzing in her ears!
   Guy Wetmore Carryl

Seeds in a dry pod, tick, tick, tick,
Tick, tick, tick like mites in a quarrel.
   Edgar Lee Masters

g

The voiced **g** is pronounced with the back of the tongue articulating against the soft palate. There is a sense of vibration on the back of the tongue.

Initial

ghee	gird	ghoul	gaga
gear	girdle	good	garner
gilt	girl	gaunt	gaudy
goiter	ghost	gruel	grail
gourd	gossip	ghastly	gown

Medial

haggle	wriggle	angled	joggle
drugs	bugle	exhaust	rogues
agog	eaglet	finger	mingled
leagues	giggle	exhibit	exit
dogs	luxurious	magnetic	auxiliary

Final

league	burgh	brig	fig
tug	shrug	egg	fugue
sprig	rug	gig	pug
brogue	dialogue	fog	shag
cog	beg	hag	gag

Consonants Combinations

a gaggle of geese	shingled dogs	vague struggle
luxurious exhibit	big leagues	drugged guard
grim greengrocer	gloomy groom	Greta glowered
glean the glen	gliding ghost	Gavin gasped

Selections for Practice

Pray the gods to intermit the plague
That needs must light on this ingratitude.
    Julius Caesar William Shakespeare

A giddy, giggling girl, her kinsfolk's plague,
Her manner vulgar, and her converse vague.
    Celia Thaxter

Aye, in the catalogue ye go for men;
As hounds and greyhounds, mongrels, spaniels, curs,
Shoughs, water rugs, and demi-wolves, are clept
All by the name of dogs.
    Macbeth William Shakespeare

MÁRGARÉT, áre you gríeving
Over Goldengrove unleaving?
Leáves, líke the things of man, you
With your fresh thoughts care for, can you?
Áh! ás the heart grows older
It will come to such sights colder
By and by, nor spare a sigh
Though worlds of wanwood leafmeal lie;
And yet you wíll weep and know why.
Now no matter, child, the name:
Sórrow's spríngs áre the same.
Nor mouth had, no nor mind, expressed
What heart heard of, ghost guessed:
It is the blight man was born for,
It is Margaret you mourn for.
    Spring and Fall Gerard Manley Hopkins

To market to market, to buy a fat pig,
Home again, home again, jiggety jig.
To market, to market, To buy a fat hog,
Home again, home again, jiggety jog.
    Mother Goose

To the glory that was Greece and the grandeur that was Rome.
    To Helen Edgar Allen Poe

He is dead and gone, lady,
He is dead and gone;

At his head a grass green turf,
At his heels a stone.

        Hamlet William Shakespeare

The Lateral Consonant

l

The consonant **l** is the only lateral consonant in English. It is made with the tip of the tongue on the gum ridge behind the upper front teeth with the sides of the tongue narrowing so that the sound of the voice can come over the sides of the tongue. The back of the tongue is touching the back molars. When the consonant **l** occurs at the beginning of a word it is lighter in tone than when it comes at the end of a word. This difference in quality is referred to as a *light* and *dark* **l** sound. These differences are generally not a problem for a native speaker of English.

    The consonant **l** can be difficult. The source of the difficulty is the tip of the tongue, which can protrude over the upper front teeth, or the at the back of the tongue, which may tense, causing a thick throaty sound or a glottal stop. Getting control of the tip of the tongue is the first step to a relaxed and resonant lateral **l** sound.

    Begin with the nasal consonant **n**. Feel the vibrations on the tip of the tongue and notice the "V" shape under the tongue. This is the muscle that controls the tip of the tongue and it should be spread slightly for **n** because the tip fans out over the gum ridge, cutting off the sound coming through the mouth and sending it through the nose. Now let the voice intone **n-n-n**. The "V" shape will narrow slightly because the sides of the tongue narrow, allowing the voice to come over the sides of the tongue. Be careful not to tense the back of the tongue and keep the tip of the tongue firmly on the gum ridge.

        l - n - l - n - l - n - l - n - l - n

        now switch to **n-l**

        n - l - n - l - n - l - n - l - n - l

1. Intone: tunnel—tunnel—tunnel—tunnel—tunnel—tunnel sounding the second syllable as one sound: **n-l**

2. Let the voice rise in pitch as you intone **l**

   Lee   lay   lie   low   Lou

3. Let the voice intone the consonant **l** at the beginning and at the end of the following words: lull   Lil   loll   Lyle   loyal

4. lily—lily—lily . . . **lllll**. Intone **l** without allowing the tip of the tongue to push forward or to pull back.

5. Let the tip of the tongue come up to the gum ridge for **l** at the end of the following words and intone the **l**. Let the pitch rise on the **l** sound at the end of the word. The back of the tongue may want to pull back, but try to focus the vibrations of the sound on the tip of the tongue. Check to see if you can see the "V" shape under the tongue, which indicates that the tip of the tongue is working. It should be a clear liquid sound.

   heal   hill   hell   Hal

Practice the following words in which **l** is at the end of the word following a vowel or diphthong. Don't let the back of the tongue push forward and don't change the shape of the vowel until the tip of the tongue comes up for the **l** sound.

iː	ɪ	e	æ	ɜː	ʌ
eel	ill	el	Al	Earl	hull
peel	bill	tell	Hal	curl	cull
Beal	fill	fell	Sal	whirl	mull
meal	till	jell	Cal	hurl	dull
weal	chill	knell	pal	twirl	lull
seal	kill	sell	gal	furl	gull

uː	ʊ	ɔː	ɑː
pool	full	all	allah
fool	pull	ball	Alia
cool	bull	fall	
ghoul	wool	call	
tool		tall	
fuel		shawl	

eɪ	aɪ	ɔɪ	oʊ	aʊ
ale	I'll	oil	pole	owl

mail	pile	royal	foal	trowel
tale	tile	soil	toll	towel
fail	file	boil	bowl	fowl
gale	guile	toil	coal	vowel
sale	while	coil	soul	jowl

It is becoming increasingly common for the diphthong **eɪ** to be shortened to just the first element **e**, which makes the word "pale" sound like "pel." Practice the difference between the short vowels **ɪ** followed by **e** and the diphthong **eɪ** followed by **l**.

ɪ-e-eɪ	ɪ-e-eɪ	ɪ-e-eɪ
pill-pell-pale	dill-dell-dale	hill-hell-hail
bill-bell-bail	nil-Nell-nail	kill-Kell-kale
mill-Mel-mail	sill-sell-sail	Jill-gel-jail
will-well-wail	shill-shell-shale	tiller-teller-tailor
till-tell-tail	fill-fell fail	Cila-cellar-sailor

Practice the difference between a long vowel or diphthong followed by the consonant **l** in a one-syllable word and a long vowel or the triphthong in a two-syllable word.

aɪl aɪəl	aʊ aʊəl	rɔɪl rɔɪəl	ʊlz ʊəlz
vile - viol	vow - vowel	roil - royal	Jules - jewels

Practice keeping the consonant **l** forward on the tip of the tongue in the following consonant combinations.

lp help, scalp, whelp, pulp, gulp, bulb, Kalb
lm film, helm, realm, elm, overwhelm
lf elf, sylph, shelf, wolf, gulf, Delft
lv twelve, delve, valve, dissolve, involve, solve
lθ wealth, filth, health, stealth
lt built, wilt, shalt, lilt, fault, adult, guilt, volt
ld field, revealed, shield, filled, walled
ldz wields, fields, shields, yields, wolds, heralds
gl eagle, giggle, haggle, bugle, juggle, struggle, goggle, burgle

clever class	glimmering glow	plastic plate
blue blossoms	flickering flame	slippery slush

The consonant **l** should be pronounced when it comes before **j**

Amelia's heliotrope	Ophelia's familiar	bilious William
brilliant cotillion	valuable stallion	Italian battalion
valiant rebellion	vermilion medallion	filial pavilion

The Syllabic l
The consonant takes the place of a vowel in an unstressed syllable:

pl	ripple, triple, apple, purple, steeple, dapple, topple, tipple
bl	scribble, scrabble, pebble, treble, gobble, squabble, marble
tl	little, brittle, rattle, cattle, mettle, settle, tattle, battle, scuttle
dl	ladle, fiddle, scandal, meddle, idle, needle, hurdle, bridle,
ndl	handle, candle, spindle, brindle, kindle, dandle
ndld	handled, dandled, kindled, fondled, bundled
nl	tonal, funnel, colonel, tunnel, fennel, panel, flannel,
sl	whistle, nestle, vessel, castle, missile, epistle, bustle, apostle
zl	perusal, frizzle, embezzle, dazzle, bamboozle, puzzle, tousle
kl	pickle, sparkle, oracle, chuckle, circle, speckle, cackle, buckle
gl	haggle, toggle, inveigle, wiggle, gargle, ogle, smuggle, burgle
fl	piffle, trifle, rueful, awful, raffle, muffle, shuffle, rifle, baffle
vl	travel, evil, drivel, carnival, revel, removal, novel, revival
θl	Ethel, methyl, brothel
ðl	betrothal
ʃl	bushel, official, crucial, commercial
ml	animal, minimal
ŋkl	wrinkle, twinkle, sprinkle, tinkle, winkle, uncle
ŋgl	strangle, bangle, dangle, bungle, jungle, mangle

little metal petal	impossible muddle	classical novel
delightful steeple	intolerable puzzle	brittle rattle
grizzled apostle	purple thistle	ample vessel

Selections for Practice
We fail?
But screw your courage to the sticking place, and we'll not fail.
    Macbeth William Shakespeare

The loveliness of loving well!
Nor would I now attempt to trace
The more than beauty of a face
Whose lineaments, upon my mind,
Are—shadows on th' unstable wind:
Thus I remember having dwelt
Some page of early lore upon,
With loitering eye, till I have felt
The letters—with their meaning—melt
To fantasies—with none.
      Tamerlane Edgar Allan Poe

You spotted snakes with double tongue,
Thorny hedgehogs, be not seen,
Newts and blind worms, do no wrong;
Come not near our fairy queen.
Philomel, with melody,
Sing in our sweet lullaby,
Lulla, lulla, lullaby; lulla, lulla, lullaby:
Never harm,
Nor quell, nor charm,
Come our lovely lady nigh;
So, good night, with lullaby.
      A Midsummer Night's Dream William Shakespeare

Hear the sledges with the bells—
Silver bells!
What a world of merriment their melody foretells!
How they tinkle, tinkle, tinkle,
In the icy air of night!
While the stars that over sprinkle
All the heavens seem to twinkle
With a crystalline delight;
Keeping time, time, time,
In a sort of Runic Rhyme

To the tintinnabulation that so musically wells
From the bells, bells, bells, bells
Bells, bells, bells—
From the jingling and the tinkling of the bells.
    The Bells Edgar Allan Poe

The Lotus blooms below the barren peak,
The Lotus blows by every winding creek;
All day the wind breathes low with mellower tone;
Through every hollow cave and alley lone
Round and round the spicy downs the yellow Lotus-dust is blown.
    The Lotus Eaters Alfred, Lord Tennyson

With love's light wings did I o'er perch these walls;
For stony limits cannot hold love out:
For what love can do, that dares love attempt;
Therefore thy kinsmen are no let to me.
    Romeo and Juliet William Shakespeare

Pale, beyond porch and portal,
Crowned with calm leaves, she stands
Who gathers all things mortal
 With cold immortal hands;
Her languid lips are sweeter
Than love's who fears to greet her
To men that mix and meet her
From many times and lands.
    The Garden of Proserpine Algernon Charles Swinburne

On a tree by a river a little tom-tit
Sang "Willow, titwillow, titwillow!"
And I said to him, "Dicky-bird, why do you sit
Singing "Willow, titwillow, titwillow?"

"Is it weakness or intellect, birdie?" I cried
"Or a rather tough worm in your little inside?"
With a shake of his poor little head, he replied,
"Oh, willow, titwillow, titwillow!"
　　　Titwillow W. S. Gilbert

The Fricative Consonants

f-v　θ-ð　s-z　ʃ-ʒ　r　h

f

The voiceless fricative consonant **f** is made with the lower lip against the upper front teeth through which the breath is released.

Initial

fee	fur	fall	foil
fit	familiar	fob	foal
fed	fun	farm	foul
fad	fool	fail	fear
fast	full	file	fire

Medial

reefer	loofah	safety	woeful
snifter	coffin	joyful	Eiffel
left	graphs	awful	offal
after	puffy	careful	duffel
surfeit	far-flung	sniffle	waffle

Final

beef	loaf	calf	wharf
sniff	fluff	cough	leaf
deaf	waif	snuff	off
gaff	hoof	cuff	turf
muff	doff	if	tough

Consonant Combinations

fee-fie-foe-fum	finally free from fear
fiddle dee dee, fiddle dee dee	fine fiddle-faddle
fifty-five fine French fillies	fined five-fifty four

Selections for Practice

Fair is foul and foul is fair;
Hover through the fog and filthy air.
> *Macbeth* William Shakespeare

The fair breeze blew, the white foam flew,
The furrow followed free;
We were the first that ever burst
Into that silent sea.
> *The Rime of the Ancient Mariner* Samuel Taylor Coleridge

My Lord, they say five moons were seen tonight;
Four fixèd, and the fifth did whirl about
The other four in wondrous motion.
> *King John* William Shakespeare

A fool, a fool! I met a fool i' the forest,
A motley fool, a miserable world!
As I do live by food I met a fool,
Who laid him down and bask'd him in the sun,
And rail'd on Lady Fortune in good terms,
In good set terms and yet a motley fool.
"Good morrow, fool," quoth I, "No sir," quoth he,
"Call me not fool till heaven hath sent me fortune."
> *As You Like It* William Shakespeare

The Thane of fife had a wife. Where is she now?
> *Macbeth* William Shakespeare

Flower in the crannied wall,
I pluck you out of the crannies,
I hold you here, root and all, in my hand,
Little flower—but if I could understand
What you are, root and all, and all in all,
I should know what God and man is.

> *Flower in the Crannied Wall* Alfred, Lord Tennyson

O Fortune, Fortune! all men call thee fickle.
If thou art fickle, what dost thou with him
That is renowned for faith? Be fickle Fortune,
For then I hope thou wilt not keep him long
But send him back again.

> *Romeo and Juliet* William Shakespeare

v

The voiced fricative consonant **v** is made with the lower lip against the upper front teeth. You should feel the vibrations of the voice on the lips and teeth. Be sure to stop the sound before you move your lips or you will get an *off-glide* "uh" sound as in "love-uh."

Initial

V	vapid	vowel	victory
vault	void	vest	view
varsity	veld	volume	vintage
vat	viscount	vicar	vast
verily	vile	veal	vote

Medial

even	avid	livid	craved
loved	believed	coven	snivels
grieves	review	valves	heaven
lavish	craven	evil	reprieved
evolve	involved	braved	review

Final

eve	live	sieve	have
alive	swerve	evolve	thrive
calve	of	shove	carve
move	drive	heave	dove
grieve	groove	slave	rove

Consonant Combinations

brief voyage	live fish	victim of love
rough voice	leave friends	live voice
safe visit	save fields	foolish vanity

Selections for Practice

Robin! Robin! Robin! All his merry thieves
Answer as the bugle note shivers through the leaves.
> "Sherwood" Alfred Noyes

Thine evil deeds are writ in gore
Nor written thus in vain—
Thy triumphs tell of fame no more
Or deepen every stain.
> *Ode to Napoleon Bonaparte* Lord Byron

Willows whiten, aspens quiver,
Little breezes dusk and shiver
Thro' the wave that runs forever
By the island in the river
Flowing down to Camelot.
> *The Lady of Shalott* Alfred, Lord Tennyson

Better it is to die, better to starve,
Than crave the hire which first we do deserve.
> *Coriolanus* William Shakespeare

Come live with me, and be my love;
And we will all the pleasures prove
That hills and valleys, dales and fields,
Woods, or steepy mountains yields.
       The Passionate Shepherd to His Love Christopher Marlowe

Adieu, and take thy praise with thee to heaven!
Thy ignominy sleep with thee in the grave,
But not remember'd in thy epitaph!
       Henry IV, 1 William Shakespeare

As he said vanity, so vain say I,
Oh! vanity, O vain all under the sky;
       The Vanity of All Worldly Things Anne Bradstreet

θ

The voiceless fricative **θ** is made with the front of the tongue against the edges of the upper front teeth. The breath is released between the teeth and the tongue.

Initial

theme	thrift	thiamine	thief
thud	through	theft	thrice
thrill	thank	throw	thousand
thirst	thigh	thimble	three
thick	throne	thought	theory

Medial

ether	depths	something	bathtub
tenths	frothing	Ethel	fifths
arithmetic	truthful	thousandths	arthritic
author	healthy	anthology	mirthful
cathedral	athletic	anything	southward

Final

sheath	twelfth	wrath	health
filth	path	myth	length
strength	sleuth	sloth	breath
dearth	doth	booth	hearth
teeth	both	north	earth

Consonants Combinations

think thin	mythical anthology	worthy author
three thousand	the thief's thumb	thrilling thought
tenth sleuth	filthy sloth	thirty-three tree
thiamin theory	healthy earth	twelfth birthday
depth and breadth	length and width	eighth hyacinth

Selections for Practice

He prayeth best who loveth best
All creatures great and small
For the dear God who loveth us
He made and loveth all.

> *The Rime of the Ancient Mariner* Samuel Taylor Coleridge

O Monstrous arrogance!
Thou liest, thou thread, thou thimble,
Thou yard, three-quarters, half yard, quarter, nail!
Thou flea, thou nit, thou winter-cricket thou!
Brav'd in mine own house with a skein of thread!
Away! thou rag, thou quantity, thou remnant
Or I shall so bemete thee with thy yard
As thou shalt think on prating whilst thou liv'st!
I tell thee, I, that thou hast marr'd her gown.

> *Taming of the Shrew* William Shakespeare

At eve the beetle boometh
Athwart the thicket line;

At noon the wild bee hummeth
About the moss'd headstone
At midnight the moon cometh,
And looketh down alone.
Her song the lintwhite swelleth,
The clear-voiced mavis dwelleth,
The callow throstle lispeth,
The slumbrous wave outwelleth
The babbling runnel cruspeth
The hollow grot replieth
Where Claribel low-lieth.

    Claribel Alfred, Lord Tennyson

First of this thing and that thing and t'other thing think.
    "Letter" Percy Bysshe Shelley

ð

The voiced fricative consonant **ð** is made with the tip of the tongue against the edges of the upper front teeth. There is a sensation of vibration on the tongue and the teeth.

Initial

thee	that	they	these
though	their	this	thou
therefore	then	those	thine
than	thus	them	there
they'll	therefore	thence	the

Medial

seething	neither	heathen	wither
leather	rather	breathing	writhing
soother	although	bother	mother
brother	father	further	either
other	bathing	loathing	gather

Final

writhe	tithe	lithe	scythe
clothe	mouthe	lathe	blithe
scathe	loathe	soothe	mouthe

Consonant Combinations
θ ð

teeth—teethe	loath—loathe	sooth—soothe
breath—breathe	sheath—sheathe	ether—either
wreath—wreathe	bath—bathe	mouth—mouthe

this thy father	bother them
those others	further tithe
thus they withered	another brother
they're loathsome	loathe thy father
seething froth	soothing bath
They sheathed the scythe	The three brothers tithed
They breathe their last breath	Thy thoughts withered

Selections for Practice

Hold thy peace, thou knave;
And I prithee hold thy peace.
    Twelfth Night William Shakespeare

Breathes there the man with soul so dead,
Who never to himself hath said,
'This is my own, my native land!'
Whose heart hath ne'er within him burn'd
As home his footsteps he hath turn'd
From wandering on a foreign strand?
    Patriotism Sir Walter Scott

How art thou out of breath, when thou hast breath
To say to me that thou art out of breath?
    Romeo and Juliet William Shakespeare

Hither and thither and whither—who knows? Who knows?
Hither and thither—but whither—who knows?
    J. F. Waller

A Being breathing thoughtful breath,
A traveler between life and death.
    She Was a Phantom of Delight William Wordsworth

There was the door to which I found no key:
There was the Veil through which I might not see:
Some little talk awhile of Me and Thee
There was—and then no more of Thee and me.
    The Rubáiyat of Omar Khayyám Edward Fitzgerald

Oh joy! that in our embers
Is something that doth live,
That nature yet remembers
What was so fugitive!
    Intimations of Immortality William Wordsworth

S Z

The consonants **s-z** are made with the teeth close together and in line, but not touching. The sides of the tongue touch and hold on to the upper molars and the tip of the tongue is free and pointing towards the front of the upper gums. The breath is directed in a thin stream against the hard surface of the upper teeth. Some students discover that they have been making the consonant **s** with the tip of the tongue behind the lower front teeth which sometimes creates a slight whistling sound called a "sibilant s."

Another common problem is using the consonant **s** instead of **z** after vowels, diphthongs and voiced consonants. When a word ending in a vowel, diphthong, or a voiced consonant is either plural or posessive and followed by an **s** at the end of a word, it is pronounced with the voiced **z**.

Example: "bees, weds, awes, is, wigs, saves, robs" all end in **z**

Note: It is possible for some people, especially those with a slightly larger tongue, to make their "s" sounds with the tip of the tongue behind the lower front teeth.

If in the opinion of your voice and speech teacher, director, or others profession-
ally competent to judge, you are able to make all the requisite sounds correctly,
you may do these exercises with the tongue behind the lower front teeth. (For
extra practice for a sibilant "s" see page 202 of Chapter VI).

s

Practice Exercises for s

To correct a sibilant or whistling "**s**" work with words of one syllable ending in
"**t**." Hold the tip of the tongue firmly against the gum ridge, then release *just the
tip* for "**s**."

Front Vowels Followed by ts

beats	meats	feats	cheats
bits	mitts	fits	chits
bets	mets	fetes	Chet's
bats	mats	fats	chats

Middle Vowels Followed by ts

hurts	curtsy	Burt's	flirts	Curt's
huts	cuts	butts	flutts	cuts

Back vowels Followed by ts

boots	loots	puts	moots	shoots
botts	lots	pots	foots	shots

It is important to develop flexibility in the tip of the tongue for the consonant **s**
sound. The tongue should move up to the gum ridge for the **s** sound before the jaw.
Practice the following words, allowing the tip of the tongue to lift up to the gum
ridge for the **t** sound *before* the jaw moves up for the release of the **s** sound.

Example: "pat" (tip of tongue up) **ts**

pats	bats	fats	gnats
hats	vats	that's	cats

tats	mats	chats	rats
slats	plaits	gats	flats

When practicing words beginning with an "**s**" bring the teeth into line without touching, let the tip of the tongue touch the gum ridge as in the "**t**" sound, then say the initial "**s**" without saying the "**t**."

t-see	t-sigh	t-say	t-soar
t-sue	t-sew	t-sow	t-sewer
t-sad	t-so	t-seer	t-sower

For words ending in "**ts**," practice bringing the tip of the tongue up to the gum ridge for the **t**, releasing the tip of the tongue for **s** from the **t**. For words ending in "**sts**" keep the teeth in line, with the tip of the tongue on the gum ridge for "**t**." Be sure that the tip of the tongue doesn't touch the back of the upper front teeth. Release the breath on the **t** right into the **s**.

ts   sts

beats	beasts	feats	feasts	bets	bests
mats	masts	pets	pests	cats	casts
fats	fasts	pats	pasts	boots	boosts
mitts	mists	hurts	Hurst's	boats	boasts
Burt's	bursts	waits	wastes	writs	wrists

Initial

sp	speed	span	spoon	spawn
	spoke	spill	spry	spite
	spine	spouse	splurge	sprout

sm	smut	smack	smelt	smock
	smoke	smut	smell	smooch
	smile	small	smog	smirch

sw	sweet	swill	swoon	swarm
	swell	switch	sweep	swim
	swain	swine	swear	swan

st	steel	still	stack	stool
	sty	step	stuck	stoop
	stood	star	stare	style

sn	sneeze	snit	snide	snore
	snipe	snip	snood	snooze
	snail	snob	snake	sniff

sl	sleep	sled	slam	slur
	slip	slide	sleek	slur
	slaw	slow	slough	slake

sk	scheme	skill	scat	scurvy
	score	scoop	scale	sky
	scar	scare	skip	skate

skw	squeeze	squall	square	squire
	squill	squeal	squab	squirm
	squib	squint	squaw	squat

str	street	strew	straw	stray
	strip	strand	stroke	stripe
	strike	strive	streak	stream

Medial

leasing	lesson	looser	pursed	burst
lisped	clasped	gasped	grasped	forceps
doom'st	alarm'st	form'st	came'st	aseptic
minced	fenced	advanced	romanced	danced
lisps	wisps	clasps	gasps	rasps
beasts	priests	masts	boasts	bursts
glistened	lessened	loosened	hastened	fastened
risks	masks	tusks	basks	disks

Final

ps	maps	snipes	coops	harps	hopes

fs	thief's	turfs	scoffs	muffs	loafs
θs	moths	births	hearths	baths	oath's
ts	streets	bites	bursts	bouts	fights
ks	peaks	dukes	crooks	lurks	aches
lps	whelps	helps	yelps	alps	scalps
lfs	sylphs	elf's	gulfs	wolf's	pelf's
dθs	widths	breadths	hundredths	thousandths	
ŋθs	lengths	strengths			
mfs	nymphs	triumphs	lymph's		
pts	conscripts	precepts	scripts	accepts	corrupts
lks	milks	whelks	sulks	silks	hulks

Selections for Practice

I saw with open eyes
Singing birds sweet
Sold in the shops
For the people to eat
Sold in the shops of
Stupidity Street.
I saw in the vision
The worm in the wheat,
And in the shops nothing for people to eat
Nothing for sale in
Stupidity Street.
  Stupidity Street Ralph Hodgson

He jests at scars that never felt a wound.
  Romeo and Juliet William Shakespeare

In sooth I know not why I am so sad.
  Merchant of Venice William Shakespeare

At length their long kiss severed, with sweet smart:
And as the last slow sudden drops are shed

From sparkling eaves when all the storm has fled,
So singly flagged the pulses of each heart.
       Nuptial Sleep Dante Gabriel Rossetti

And thou, who didst the stars and sunbeams know,
Self-schooled, self-scanned, self-honoured, self-secure,
Didst tread on earth unguessed at. Better so!
All pains the immortal spirit must endure,
All weakness that impairs, all griefs that bow,
Find their sole voice in that victorious brow.
       Shakespeare Matthew Arnold

Apes and monkeys, twixst two such shes,
Would chatter this way and contemn with mows the other.
       Cymbeline William Shakespeare

Some love too little, some too long
Some sell and other's buy;
Some do the deed with many tears,
And some without a sigh:
For each man kills the thing he loves,
Yet each man does not die.
       The Ballad of Reading Gaol Oscar Wilde

Rats!
They fought the dogs and killed the cats,
And bit the babies in the cradles,
And ate the cheeses out of the vats,
And licked the soup from the cooks own ladles,
Split open the kegs of salted sprats,
 Made nests inside men's Sunday hats,
And even spoiled the women's chats,
By drowning their speaking
With shrieking and squeaking
In fifty different sharps and flats.
       The Pied Piper of Hamlin Robert Browning

Success is counted sweetest
By those who ne 'er succeed.
To comprehend a nectar
Requires sorest need.
                Emily Dickinson

The mast-beater blows.
The bow chisels
the smooth sea
Into spraystorms:
The wild willow-shaker
Whirls hard and cold,
Savaging the breast
Of my sailing swan.
                Egil's Saga 1230 AD Anonymous

If wishes were horses, beggars would ride,
If turnips were watches, I would wear one by my side
And if "ifs" and "ands" were pots and pans
There'd be no work for tinkers!
                Mother Goose

Thou still unravish'd bride of quietness
Thou foster-child of silence and slow time,
Sylvan historian, who canst thus express
A flowery tale more sweetly than our rhyme.
                Ode on a Grecian Urn John Keats

But it is I
That, lying by the violet in the sun,
Do as the carrion does, not as the flower,
Corrupt with virtuous season. Can it be
That modesty may more betray our sense
Than woman's lightness?
                Measure for Measure William Shakespeare

z

The consonant **z** is produced in the same manner as the consonant **s** except that it is voiced. The teeth are in alignment and the tip of the tongue is pointing toward the front of the upper gum ridge. There is a sensation of vibration on the tip of the tongue.

Initial

zeal	zoo	zap	zillion
zip	zounds	zealot	zircon
zest	zone	zed	zither
Zanzibar	Zane	zenith	zodiac
Zachary	zany	zinc	zombie

Medial

buzzed	puzzle	poison	muslin
mused	crazy	muzzle	fizzy
pleased	reason	weasel	buzzard
easy	Ezra	drizzle	perusal
cousin	muesli	resin	deserve

Final

appease	lauds	bulbs	ribbons
daubs	yawns	films	gobbles
looms	hails	elves	animals
halves	leagues	fiends	softens
oaths	pangs	sharpens	baffles

Consonant Combinations

Ethel's raffles	bamboozles couples
It's Mitchel's	commands fiends
people's riddles	embezzles trifles
citizens examples	enlivens seasons

Voiced Consonants and Vowels Followed by z

bz	mz	vz	ðz	dz	lz
ribs	sums	loves	breathes	odes	eels
cabs	wombs	raves	bathes	reed	earls
sobs	forms	hooves	teethes	bids	ails
verbs	seems	lives	wreathes	roads	oils
orbs	homes	curves	oaths	gods	owls
snobs	limbs	weaves	sheathes	lauds	aisles

nz	dʒɪz	sɪz	zɪz	gz	ŋz
leans	judges	kisses	freezes	bags	rings
grins	badges	masses	loses	figs	hangs
loans	cages	losses	praises	drugs	kings
fawns	ledges	cases	sneezes	legs	lungs
loins	sledges	classes	clauses	begs	bangs
fans	ridges	tosses	sizes	hogs	longs

z and Syllabic Consonants

zm	zn	zl	pnz	plz	bnz
atheism	season	easel	ripens	peoples	ribbons
criticism	resin	fizzle	deepens	cripples	carbons
witticism	prison	embezzle	opens	apples	bobbins

blz	fnz	vlz	tnz	dlz	sns
scribbles	stiffens	snivels	sweetens	needles	listens
bubbles	coffins	rivals	fattens	riddles	moistens
foibles	siphons	travels	shortens	saddles	glistens

slz	znz	zlz	knz	klz	tʃnz
epistles	reasons	weasels	thickens	pickles	kitchens
castles	poisons	frazzles	darkens	circles	urchins
nestles	raisins	puzzles	awakens	cackles	luncheons

Selections for Practice
But now farewell. I am going a long way
With these thou seëst—if indeed I go—

(For all my mind is clouded with a doubt)
To the island-valley of Avilion;
Where falls not hail, or rain, or any snow,
Nor ever wind blows loudly; but it lies
Deep-meadow'd, happy, fair with orchard-lawns
And bowery hollows crown'd with summer sea,
Where I will heal me of my grievous wound.
Idylls of the King Alfred Lord Tennyson

For winter's rain's and ruins are over,
And all the season of snows and sins:
The days dividing lover and lover,
The light that loses, the night that wins;
And time remembered is grief forgotten,
And frosts are slain and flowers begotten,
And in green underwood and cover,
Blossom by blossom the spring begins.
Atalanta in Calydon Algernon Charles Swinburne

Needles and pins, needles and pins,
When a man marries his trouble begins.
Mother Goose

Music that gentlier on the spirit lies,
Than tired eyelids upon tired eyes;
Music that brings sweet sleep down from the blissful skies.
The Song of the Lotus-Eaters Alfred, Lord Tennyson

We are the music makers,
And we are the dreamers of dreams,
Wandering by lone sea-breakers,
And sitting by desolate streams;
World-losers and world forsakers,
On whom the pale moon gleams:

Yet we are the movers and shakers
Of the world for ever, it seems.
      Ode A.W.E. O'Shaugnessy

Stiffen the sinews, summon up the blood,
Disguise fair nature with hard-favour'd rage;
      Henry V William Shakespeare

ʃ

The voiceless fricative ʃ is made with the tip of the tongue pointing towards the *middle* of the gum ridge with the sides of the tongue touching the upper molars. The lips do *not* protrude.

Initial

she	shoe	shame	share
ship	Shule	shale	shake
shell	shoot	shade	shower
sham	shock	shy	shoal
shaft	shan't	shawl	shiver

Medial

cushion	Russian	machine	passion
anxious	washed	fissure	ocean
bushel	racial	mention	ration
conscience	national	vacation	fished
vicious	session	partial	washed

Final

push	wish	bash	hush
mash	leash	flesh	gouache
harsh	wash	shush	cash
nosh	Welsh	fish	bush
trash	French	bash	hash

Consonant Combinations

Note: Do not add the consonant **s** between two words in which the first ends in **t** and the second begins with a **j** as in "want you" making them sounds like "want chew."

want you	didn't you	shouldn't you
don't you	couldn't you	won't you
hadn't you	wouldn't you	can't you

Selections for Practice

The sixth age shifts
Into the lean and slippered pantaloon
With spectacles on nose and pouch on side;
His youthful hose well saved, a world too wide
For his shrunk shank, and his big manly voice,
Turning again toward childish treble, pipes
And whistles in his sound. Last scene of all,
That ends this strange eventful history,
Is second childishness and mere oblivion—
Sans teeth, sans eyes, sans taste, sans everything.
  As You Like It William Shakespeare

At the outset I may mention it's my sovereign intention
To revive the classic memories of Athens at its best.
For the company possesses all the necessary dresses
And a course of quiet cramming will supply us with the rest.
  The Grand Duke W. S. Gilbert

Tush, tush! fear boys with bugs.
  The Taming of the Shrew William Shakespeare

And ever and anon with host to host
Shocks and the splintering spear, the hard mail hewn,
Shield breakings, and the clash of brands, and the crash

Of battle-axes on shattered helms and shrieks,
Shouts of heathen and the traitor Knights.
    Idylls of the King Alfred, Lord Tennyson

Beyond the shadow of the ship
I watched the water-snakes:
They moved in tracks of shining white,
And when they reared, the elfish light
Fell off in hoary flakes
Within the shadow of the ship
I watched their rich attire,
They coiled and swam; and every track
Was a flash of golden fire.
   The Rime of the Ancient Mariner Samuel Taylor Coleridge

3

The voiced fricative **ʒ** like, the voiceless **ʃ**, is made with the tip of the tongue pointing towards the *middle* of the gum ridge with the sides of the tongue touching the upper molars. The sound vibrates on the tip of the tongue and the lips do *not* protrude.

Initial

There are no words in English that begin with the **ʒ** sound, however it is very common in French.

  Example: Jean, George, Germaine, Jacques, Jules.

Medial

azure	usual	explosion	usurer
negligee	lingerie	seizure	visionary
treasure	vision	persuasion	intrusion
envision	Persian	leisure	regime
illusion	treasurer	rouged	pleasure

Final

prestige	camouflage	massage	rouge
corsage	espionage	badinage	garage
triage	mirage	cortege	beige

Consonant Combinations

Aleutian illusion	casual pleasure
azure corsage	envisioned explosion
Persian invasion	pleasurable espionage

Note: Don't substitute the **ʒ** sound before **j** in the following combinations, as in "did jew."

did you	would you	should you	could you
had you	bid you	rid you	said you

Selections for Practice

Haste still pays haste, and leisure answers leisure,
Like doth quit like, and measure still for measure.
　　　　Measure for Measure William Shakespeare

Bacchus' blessings are a treasure,
Drinking is the solders' pleasure:
Rich the treasure, sweet the pleasure,
Sweet is pleasure after pain.
　　　　"Alexander's Feast" John Dryden

Lay not up for yourself treasures upon earth,
But lay up for yourself treasures in heaven.
For where your treasure is,
here will your heart be also.
　　　　The Book of Matthew

Peace, ho! I bar confusion
'Tis I must make conclusion
Of these most strange events.
　　　　As You Like It William Shakespeare

Every moment brings a treasure
Of its own especial pleasure.
Though the moments quickly die,
Greet them gaily as they fly…
Let us gaily tread the measure,
Make the most of fleeting leisure;
  The Pirates of Penzance W. S. Gilbert

And still she slept and azure-lidded sleep,
In blanched linen, smooth, and lavendered,
While he from forth the closet brought a heap
Of candied apple, quince, and plum and gourd;
  The Eve of St. Agnes John Keats

r

The consonant **r** is made with the tip of the tongue free and pointing toward the back of the upper gum ridge. The sides of the tongue are touching the back molars and the voice seems to be vibrating just behind the hard palate.

Don't let the lips form the **r** sound in any way. One of the most common speech problems with the consonant **r** is when the sound is made with the lips rather than with the tip of the tongue. In an exaggerated form this would make the phrase "red river" sound like "wed wiver."

The consonant **r** is pronounced *only* if it is followed by a vowel or a diphthong.

Initial

reap	rip	rent	rap	run	ruse
read	writ	red	ram	rut	rube
real	rift	realm	raft	rush	roof
wreath	wrist	wreck	wrath	runt	rule
rookery	rear	roar	romantic	rye	rot
rook	rare	revile	rotund	Roy	rock
rookie	Rhur	rout	raw	raven	rondo

Medial

Practice the consonant **r** between the following vowel sounds:

ɪr	er	ær	ɔːr
eruption	peril	parable	oral
mirror	terror	marry	forum
heroic	America	caramel	glory

ɑːr	ɜːr	ər	ʌr
starry	furry	arise	turret
aria	worry	career	thorough
Bari	blurring	arena	current
tarry	scurrilous	parade	hurry

aɪr	ɪɚr	ɛɚr	ʊɚr
wiry	Erie	airy	rural
Irish	dreary	Mary	during
irony	herein	vary	curious
fiery	period	chary	perjury

Linking r

When a word ends in **r** and the word that follows begins with a vowel or a diphthongs then the **r** is pronounced and elided into the following word as in "or else."

Far away	wear out	our own
over all	sister of	for ever
tear up	clear off	near east
ginger ale	pair of	o'er all

Final

When the consonant **r** comes at the end of a word, try not to pull the tongue too far back and over pronounce the final **r** using tension in the back of the tongue.

bar	tore	fur	leer
mere	ear	hour	chair
fair	poor	stare	core
tire	floor	clear	store
rear	jar	door	mar

R Coloration

In a word with an **r** in the spelling followed by another consonant in the same syllable, as in the word "hard," the **r** can be "colored" or indicated by a slight inflection without pulling the tongue back or inverting it. This is often used when performing classic plays in which no regional accent is indicated. To color an **r**, relax the tongue—the flatter the tongue the less of an **r** sound there will be.

Note: In R. P. (British Standard Speech), the **r** is eliminated entirely before another consonant unless the following word begins with a vowel.

Practice r Coloration

dark barn	more charm	learn art
start turning	charming clerk	farm cart
art course	warm heart	art work

Consonant Combinations with r

Practice the consonant **r** when it is preceded by the following consonants:

pr	**br**
previous practice	brief brawl
presidential pride	brilliant bronzes
practical proportion	broken bracelets

fr	**θr**
frantic Friday	three thrones
fresh frozen fruit	thrilling throats
free French fries	thrice three

tr	**dr**
truly tragic truce	dreadful Druids
translated tract	dreary drama
tropic trademark	drowsy dryad

ʃr	**kr**
shredded shrimp	crafty crook
shrill shrew	crawling crabs
shriven shroud	crooked crown

str	**gr**
strange strife	green grocer
stricken structure	grim graduate
streaming streets	groggy gremlin
spr	**skr**
spread of sprats	scribbled scrawl
spreading spruce	scratched screen
sprinkling spring	scrubby scrap

Tongue Twisters

Round the rough and rugged rock the ragged rascal ran.
Round and round the great arena roared the Roman charioteers.

Selections for Practice

She only said, "My life is dreary,
He cometh not," she said; She said,
"I am aweary, aweary,
I would that I were dead!"
          Mariana Alfred, Lord Tennyson

Roll on, thou deep and dark blue ocean, roll!
          Child Harold's Pilgrimage, IV Lord Byron

You heard as if an army muttered,
And the muttering grew to a grumbling;
 And the grumbling grew to a mighty rumbling;
And out of the houses the rats came tumbling
Great rats, small rats, lean rats, brawny rats,
Brown rats, black rats, gray rats, tawny rats,
Grave old plodders, gay young friskers,
Fathers, mothers, uncles, cousins,
Cocking tails and pricking whiskers,
Families by tens and dozens,

Brothers, sisters, husbands, wives—
Followed the piper for their lives.
      The Pied Piper of Hamelin   Robert Browning

The moving finger writes; and having writ,
Moves on; nor all your piety nor wit
Shall lure it back to cancel half a line,
Nor all your Tears wash out a Word of it.
      The Rubáiyat of Omar Khayyám   Edward Fitzgerald

The road was a ribbon of moonlight over the purple moor,
And the highwayman came riding—riding—riding
The highwayman came riding, up to the old inn-door.
      The Highwayman   Alfred Noyes

h

The voiced and voiceless fricative **h** is a puff of breath released from the back of the throat. When it is voiceless, it always occurs at the *beginning* of a word. It is slightly voiced **ɦ** when it occurs in the *middle* of a word.

Initial

he	who	her	hoist
hymn	hood	hurl	hope
head	Homer	hut	how
hat	haul	hay	here
half	haughty	high	hotel

Medial

apprehensive	behind	grasshopper	inhuman
inhabit	ahead	behold	inherit
Ohio	mohair	mahogany	behemoth
rehearsal	inhibited	Jehovah	apprehend
perhaps	behavior	withhold	menhir
ahoy	unhappy	Bahamas	inhumane

This sound does not occur in a final position.

Note: In compound words when "h" begins the second syllable, the "h" is often omitted.

   Example:
      shepherd   vehicle   forehead   gingham
      Durham   Chatham   Wickham   Gorham

Note: There are words beginning with "**h**" in the spelling which are pronounced with the **h** sound in British English, but dropped in American English. Apparently it was the fashion to drop "h's" in the 18th Century, and while the British put the **h** back in their pronunciation, Americans still drop it. Remember to put the **h** in these words if you are in a play requiring a British accent using R.P. (Received Pronunciation).

      Examples: herb, herbal, homage

Note: In the words "honor, hour, honorable, honest," the **h** is always dropped.

Consonant Combinations

apprehensive hemisphere   Helen's horoscope
healthy inhabitants   hostile handling
Ohio ahead   her Hartford home
inhibited behavior   horrible grasshopper

Selections for Practice

Heigh ho! sing heigh ho! unto the green holly
Most friendship is feigning, most loving mere folly:
Then, heigh ho, the holly!
This life is most jolly.
      As You Like It William Shakespeare

Hence! home, you idle creatures, get you home:
Is this a holiday? What know you not,
Being mechanical, you ought not walk
Upon a labouring day without the sign
Of your profession? Speak, what trade art thou?
      Julius Caesar William Shakespeare

Waken, lords and ladies gay,
On the mountain dawns the day,
All the jolly chase is here,
With hawk and horse and hunting spear!
Hounds are in their couples yelling,
Hawks are whistling, horns are knelling,
Merrily, merrily, mingle they
Waken, lords and ladies gay.
>   *Hunting Song* Sir Walter Scott

What, should I hurt her, strike her, kill her dead?
Although I hate her, I'll not harm her so.
>   *A Midsummer Night's Dream* William Shakespeare

My heart's in the Highlands, my heart is not here;
My heart's in the Highlands a chasing the deer.
A chasing the wild deer, and following the roe,
My heart's in the Highlands, wherever I go.
>   *My Heart's in the Highlands* Robert Burns

This be the verse you grave for me:
Here he lies where he long'd to be;
Home is the sailor, home from the sea,
And the hunter home from the hill.
>   *Requiem* Robert Louis Stevenson

The Glides

ʍ w j

A glide is a consonant that begins in one position and then moves into another.
There are *three* glides in English.

The voiced and voiceless Glides ʍ w are formed by the lips in the rounded
position for the back vowel **u:** (who). For the voiceless consonant ʍ, which is
always spelled with a "wh" sound, round your lips and then blow, gliding into the
neutral position.

Initial

W

wean	waft	way	weir
weak	were	wide	wary
will	wench	wain	wiry
weld	worm	waistcoat	wooer
welkin	worst	weary	woe

ᴍ

where	wham	whist	while
which	whoa	whip	whiskey
whim	whisker	whale	whelk

Medial

W

beware	quote	quarry	squirrel
queer	quip	quarrel	dimwit
quirk	quart	equal	squaw
queen	acquit	quarto	equip
aqua	acquire	quiz	queasy

ᴍ

awhile	nowhere	overwhelm
somewhere	anywhere	erstwhile
meanwhile	elsewhere	underwhelm

This sound does not occur in a final position.

Practice the contrast between the voiceless and voiced consonants ᴍ W

whee—we	where—wear
which—witch	why—Y
whet—wet	whether—weather
when—wen	whey—way
whack—WAC	wherry—wary
whirr—were	whit—wit

Consonant Combinations

where will you wait
which way will we row
which white wine
Where will you wear it

Will's white whippet
weary wheelwright's wit
what will William acquire
Walter was acquainted

Tongue Twister

Whether the weather be fine
Or whether the weather be not
Whether the weather be cold
Or whether the weather be hot.
We'll weather the weather
Whatever the weather,
Whether we like it or not.

> Anonymous

Selections for Practice

…I know not what I am
Nor whence I came, nor whether I be King.

> *Idylls of the King* Alfred, Lord Tennyson

The mad old witch wife wailed and wept.

> *The Faerie Queen* Edmund Spenser

There was a dwelling of Kings
Ere the world was waxen old;
Dukes were the door-wards there,
And the roofs were thatched with gold;
Earls were the wrights that wrought it,
And silver nailed its doors;
Earls' wives were the weaving women,
Queens' daughters strewed its floors.
And the masters of its song-craft
Were the mightiest men that cast

The sails of the storm of battle
Adown the bickering blast.
> *The Story of Sigurd the Volsung* William Morris

Whirl up, sea—
whirl your pointed pines,
splash your great pines
on our rocks,
hurl your green over us,
cover us with your pools of fir.
> *Oread* H.D.

A man that had a wife with such a wit, he might say,
Wit, whither wilt?
> *As You Like It* William Shakespeare

These are but wild and whirling words, my lord.
> *Hamlet* William Shakespeare

Who, every word by all my wit being scann'd,
Wants wit in all one word to understand.
> *The Comedy of Errors* William Shakespeare

The sea awoke at midnight from its sleep,
And round the pebbly beaches far and wide
I heard the first wave of the rising tide
Rush onward with uninterrupted sweep.
> *The Sound of the Sea* Henry Wadsworth Longfellow

j

The consonant **j** is made with the tip of the tongue behind the lower front teeth
and the front of the tongue arching up toward the hard palate as if for the first
front vowel **iː**.

Initial

ye	Yule	your	Yiddish
you	yea	yet	yawn
unite	yam	Yalta	Europe
yank	yore	yarn	yak
year	yeast	young	Yarmouth

Medial

Students often find **j** difficult after certain consonants, although this is mainly a problem of familiarity with the pronunciation of the word rather than actual difficulty with the sound. The same student who hesitates over "new" has no difficulty at all saying "few."

pew	debut	view	prelude
mute	new	dual	during
avenue	neutral	volume	obtuse
value	renew	Neptune	endure
student	nude	costume	futile
duel	adieu	duet	tumult
stupid	institute	hirsute	dues
duke	opportunity	hew	dew
mutability	ducal	duality	newt

This sound does not occur in a final position.

Selections for Practice

Oliver: Good Monsieur Charles, what's the new news at the new court?
Charles: There's no news at the court sir, but the old news: that is, the old Duke, is banished by his younger brother, the new Duke, and three or four loving lords have put themselves into voluntary exile with him, whose lands and revenues enrich the new Duke. Therefore he gives them good leave to wander.

    As You Like It William Shakespeare

And thus yieldeth the year to yesterday's many.
    The Bruce John Barbour

Yield, yield, ye youths! Ye yeoman, yield your yell.
   "The Siege of Belgrade"

What occupation do you there pursue?
This is a lonesome place for one like you.
      Resolution and Independence William Wordsworth

So nigh is grandeur to our dust,
So near is God to man.
When duty whispers low, "Thou must,"
The youth replies, "I can."
      Voluntaries Ralph Waldo Emerson

News, news, news, my gossiping friends,
I have wonderful news to tell,
A lady by me her compliments sends;
And this is the news from Hell.
      News Owen Meredith

The Affricates

tʃ dʒ

Affricates are two consonants blended together to form one sound.
   The voiceless affricate **tʃ** is made with the tip of the tongue on the gum ridge for **t**, then the breath is released with the tip of the tongue for the **ʃ** sound creating a blend of **tʃ**.

Initial

cheap	church	chew	chest
cheese	churn	choose	chat
cheek	churl	chalk	cheer
chip	chubby	chocolate	chow
cheddar	chunk	chime	chair

Medial

bleached	pinched	launched	crunched
pitched	etched	catcher	wrenched
culture	factual	scorched	marched
mixture	arched	watched	archery
rapture	perched	Richard	rapture

Final

pitch	fetch	starch	catch
batch	thatch	search	pitch
much	touch	arch	rich
watch	Dutch	crutch	munch
which	lunch	hutch	stretch

Consonant Combinations

munched chunky cheddar cheese

cheeky chubby Dutch butcher

scorched bleached churn

which rich orchard

Richard's luncheon

choose Dutch chocolate

Richard searched the church

cheap Chinese chain

thatched birch

catch that batch

Selections for Practice

A sailor's wife had chestnuts in her lap,
And munch'd and munch'd and munch'd.
    Macbeth William Shakespeare

Urge neither charity nor shame to me:
Uncharitably with me have you dealt,
And shamefully my hopes by you are butcher'd.
My charity is outrage, life my shame;
And in that shame still live my sorrow's rage!
    Richard III William Shakespeare

When I was a child, I spake as a child,
I understood as a child, I thought as a child;
But when I became a man, I put away childish things.
          St. Paul to the Corinthians

No? when Nature hath made a fair creature, May she not by Fortune fall into the fire? though Nature hath given us wit to flout at Fortune, hath not Fortune sent in this fool to Cut off argument?
          As You Like It William Shakespeare

Then I said "I covet truth;
Beauty is unripe childhood's cheat;
I leave it behind with the games of youth."
          "Each and All" Ralph Waldo Emerson

Here feel we but the penalty of Adam,
The season's difference; as the icy fang
And churlish chiding of the winter's wind...
          As You Like It William Shakespeare

dʒ

The voiced affricate **dʒ** is made with the tip of the tongue on the gum ridge in the position for **d** and the sound is released on **j**. There is a sensation of vibration on the gum ridge and tongue. Don't stop the voice before the sound is completed.

Initial

jeep	jewel	jive	Jean
jig	jaw	jowl	germ
jasper	joy	juniper	gibe
genuine	Japan	Java	June
jazz	jug	jump	gentleman

Medial

adjourn	pillaged	adjust	fragile
regiment	congeal	badger	budget
courageous	magician	wedged	charged
foraged	voyager	schedule	urged
cudgel	gadget	marriages	lounged

Final

page	forge	pledge	liege
budge	merge	wage	bridge
verge	fudge	dredge	gorge
trudge	nudge	lunge	oblige
judge	engage	rage	porridge

Consonant Combinations

jump, Jenny, jump

congealed jasper jelly

obliging engaged pledge

genuine badger's jaw

John enjoyed Java's jungle

dredge the sludge

courageous magician

general's aging regiment

Selections for Practice

Judge not that ye be not judged.
For with what judgment we judge, ye shall be judged;
and with what measure ye mete, it shall be measured to you again.
The Book of Matthew

Jenny kiss'd me when we met,
Jumping from the chair she sat in;
Time, you thief, who love to get
Sweets into your list, Put that in.
Say I'm weary, say I'm sad,
Say that health and wealth have missed me,
Say I'm growing old, but add, Jenny kissed me.
Jenny Kissed Me Leigh Hunt

Therefore, Jew,
Though justice be thy plea, consider this,
That, in the course of justice, none of us
Should see salvation.
> *The Merchant of Venice* William Shakespeare

I envy not in any moods
The captive void of noble rage,
The linnet born within the cage,
That never knew the summer's woods.
> *In Memoriam* Alfred, Lord Tennyson

Imagination gathers up
The undiscovered Universe,
Like jewels in a jasper cup.
> *Imagination* John Davidson

Silence augmenteth grief, writing increaseth rage,
Staled are my thoughts, which loved and lost the wonder of our age:
Yet quickened now with fire, though dead with frost ere now,
Enraged I write I know not what; dead, quick, I know not how.
> *Epitaph on Sir Phillip Sidney* Fulke Greville, Lord Brooke

The English Vowel Sounds

The Front Vowels

iː *Key Vowel*

iː	we
ɪ	will
e	let
æ	Ann
a	pass

Begin with a slight smile, this will bring the jaw up. Keep the tip of the tongue behind the lower front teeth with the front of the tongue arching forward. Don't tense the jaw or the lips. Remember **iː** is your *key vowel* and determines the shape of the succeeding front vowels.

iː
Initial

eve	eke	eel	east
eat	each	even	Eden
ether	ease	equal	eagle
e'en	either	Ibo	equality
equinox	equine	eradiate	Esau

Medial

heave	beam	thieve	seethe
weed	careen	veal	pea
wheeze	league	being	cedar
reef	heath	peat	geese
beak	cheek	tureen	knead

Final

me	see	free	lea
pea	be	knee	agree
ye	she	he	guarantee
key	fee	thee	tea
Dee	quay	plea	spree

Phrases for Practice

leave three trees
seize the dream machine
please don't tease the weasel
even he will be free
clean meandering streams

tea for three please
congealed eels are appealing
keep mean bees in trees
beat a retreat
free treats at sea

Selections for Practice

He came and took me by the hand
Up to a red rose tree,
He kept his meaning to Himself

But he gave a rose to me,
I did not pray Him to lay bare
That mystery to me,
Enough that the rose was Heaven to smell,
And His own face to see.
              "The Mystery" Ralph Hodgson

Her pretty feet
Like snails did creep
A little out, and then,
As if they playèd at bo-peep,
Did soon draw in again.
              Upon Her Feet Robert Herrick

And here's the happy bounding flea—
You cannot tell the he from she.
The sexes look alike, you see;
But she can tell, and so can he.
              The Flea Roland Young

To make a prairie it takes a clover and one bee,
One clover, and a bee,
And revery.
The revery alone will do,
If bees are few.
              Emily Dickinson

Waking or asleep
Thou of death must deem
Things more true and deep
Than we mortals dream
Or how could thy notes flow in such a crystal stream?
              To a Skylark Percy Bysshe Shelley

O sleep, o gentle sleep,
Nature's soft nurse. How have I frighted thee
That thou, no more will weigh my eyelids down
 And steep my senses in forgetfulness.
        Henry IV, Part 2 William Shakespeare

While the earth remaineth, seedtime and harvest, and cold and heat, and summer and winter, and day and night shall not cease.
        Genesis 4:21

O My Dark Rosaleen,
Do not sigh, do not weep!
The priests are on the ocean green,
 They march along the deep,
There's wine from the royal Pope,
Upon the ocean green;
And Spanish ale shall give you hope,
My Dark Rosaleen!
My own Rosaleen!
Shall glad your heart, shall give you hope,
Shall give you health, and help and hope,
My Dark Rosaleen!
        Dark Rosaleen James Clarence Mangan

For such a tide as moving seems asleep,
Too full for sound and foam,
When that which drew from out the boundless deep
Turns again home.
        Crossing the Bar Alfred, Lord Tennyson

ɪ

For the second front vowel **ɪ** drop the jaw a little and keep the lips slightly spread.

Initial

if	it	is	ill
imagine	enough	exist	eternal
illegal	Italy	ilk	ibid
itch	England	exact	Ibsen
Ithaca	in	employ	irritate

Medial

pin	been	fill	din
sin	kin	villain	thin
lily	zinc	silly	giddy
gin	this	witty	seduce
miss	pick	bring	niche

Final

Most words with suffixes ending in "y" are pronounced with the very short **iː**, but in rapid connected speech they can be pronounced with **I**, especially in R.P.

happily	worry	merry	silly
arbitrary	really	ability	pity
formerly	angrily	surely	dignity
family	eternity	comely	piety
poetry	quantity	homily	velocity

Phrases for Practice

a bit dim	this is a big city
it's dimly lit	a bit silly
average marriage	eligible women
it's a little crooked	blameless princess

The second front vowel **I** should always be short in the following prefixes and suffixes:

Prefixes

imagine	beloved	debate	serene
enough	before	deny	severe

evade	believe	delight	seclude
eternity	begin	deposit	select
emotion	because	destroy	seduce
retire	expand	exact	preclude
return	expect	examine	prescribe
release	example	exist	predict
reform	experience	extent	prevail
rehearse	explode	exhaust	precede

Suffixes

blameless	toneless	lawless	formless
coldness	heartless	bitterness	darkness
harmless	falseness	wickedness	lightness
goodness	dreamless	righteousness	doubtless
breathless	thoughtless	harshness	blindness

Phrases for Practice

she projected bitterness

the subject was marriage

projected wickedness

to retard flames

subjected to disease

the rejected princess

a private project

the object of lawlessness

perfect righteousness

reject the glasses

Selections for Practice

Alas for the rarity

Of Christian charity

Under the sun!

Oh! it was pitiful!

Near a whole city full,

Home she had none.

The Bridge of Sighs Thomas Hood

And the raven never flitting,

Still is sitting, still is sitting

On the pallid bust of Pallas
Just above my chamber door.
          The Raven Edgar Allen Poe

What pleasure hast thou of thy changeless bliss?
Nay, if love lasted, there were joy in this;
But life's way is the wind's way, all these things
Are but brief voices breathed on shifting strings.
          "The Light of Asia" Edwin Arnold

The year's at the spring
And day's at the morn'
Morning's at seven;
The hill-side's dew pearled;
The lark's on the wing;
The snail's on the thorn;
God's in his heaven—
All's right with the world.
          Pippa Passes Robert Browning

Here's a first-rate opportunity
To get married with impunity
To indulge in the felicity
Of unbounded domesticity.
You shall quickly be personified,
Conjugally matrimonified,
By a doctor of divinity,
Who resides in this vicinity.
          The Pirates of Penzance W. S. Gilbert

Across the narrow beach we flit.
One little sand-piper and I;
And fast I gather, bit by bit,
The scattered drift-wood, bleached and dry.

The wild waves reach their hands for it,
The wild wind raves, the tide runs high,
And up and down the beach we flit,
One little sand-piper and I.
  The Sand-Piper Celia Laighton Thaxter

e
For the third front vowel **e** drop the jaw again with the lips slightly spread.

Initial

edge	elf	elegant	everywhere
elephant	any	Edward	engine
emblem	ebb	enemy	end
egg	Ethel	empty	ethics
extra	expect	etch	echo

Medial

again	went	bend	lemon
strength	thread	gem	shed
deaf	led	kettle	pen
mesh	pleasure	knell	guess
reddish	berry	measure	twenty

This sound does not occur in a final ending.

Prefixes with e *or* ɪ
The prefix "ex" can be pronounced with either **e** or **ɪ**. No rule always applies, except usage. When in doubt consult a dictionary. Here are some words in general use.

ɪ		**e**	
exact	excuse	extent	excerpt
exam	excite	exile	exit
exceed	except	exorcism	expedite
excrete	example	extract	expert
expel	excess	execute	extirpation

Suffixes with e *or* ı

Note: The following words change in pronunciation from ı to e according to the meaning of the word and whether the word is a verb, adverb, noun or adjective, Verbs and adverbs are generally pronounced with e and nouns and adjectives with ı but there are exceptions. Again, when in doubt consult a dictionary.

object, perfect, subject

e
Verb

object	I object to this.	
	objectionable	objectively
	objection	objector
	objective	objectivity

perfect	She tried to perfect the mechanism.
	perfectible
	perfection
	perfectionist

subject	He was made to subject to the treaty.
	subjection
	subjective
	subjected

ı
Noun, Adjective or Adverb

object	She was the object of his affection.
perfect	It's the perfect dress.
subject	Happiness was the subject of the sentence.

Phrases for Practice

Evelyn lent Ben ten pens

Ben lent Tim's pen

Wendy etched twenty lemons

Emma sent Edward ten eggs

the rent is seventy-seven cents   Betty's red elephant, Ethel
Defend Teddy's pet terrier   Don't forget Chester's deaf

The fourth front vowel **ɛ** is not used in American English except as the first element of the diphthong **ɛɹ** as in "air," however it is used in some dialects in the North of England and in Ireland and Scotland as a substitute for the third front vowel **e**.

Selections for Practice

Oh! My name is John Wellington Wells,
I'm a dealer in magic and spells,
In blessings and curses
And ever-filled purses,
In prophecies, witches and knells…
        The Sorcerer   W. S. Gilbert

Tell me where is Fancy bred,
Or in the heart, or in the head?
How begot, how nourished?
Reply, reply.
It is engender 'd in the eyes:
With gazing fed; and Fancy dies
In the cradle where it lies.
Let us all ring Fancy's knell;
I'll begin it:—Ding, dong, bell
—Ding, dong, bell
        The Merchant of Venice   William Shakespeare

The rain to the wind said,
"You push and I'll pelt."
They so smote the garden bed
That the flowers actually knelt,
And lay lodged—though not dead,
I know how the flowers felt.
        Robert Frost

I do not like thee, Doctor Fell;
The reason why I cannot tell;
But this I know, and know full well,
I do not like thee, Doctor Fell.
        Mother Goose

…The bell invites me.
Hear it not, Duncan; for it is a knell
That summons thee to heaven or to hell.
        Macbeth William Shakespeare

There was an Old Man of Kilkenny,
Who never had more than a penny;
He spent all that money in onions and honey,
That wayward Old Man of Kilkenny
        Book of Nonsense Edward Lear

æ
For the fifth front vowel **æ** the lips are slightly spread and the jaw has dropped slightly form the preceding vowel sound.

Initial

apple	arid	average	amble
am	arras	Ann	Andrew
azure	arable	actor	aster
aspirin	arrow	abbot	at
afghan	arrogant	abcess	absent

Medial

labyrinth	dad	pants	tramp
caramel	grand	mustache	parasite
farrow	raffle	Harold	marigold
harass	lavish	parasol	carry
national	brand	marry	character

This sound does not occur in a final position.

Phrases for Practice

fastened plastic bag
barren national landscape
scratch the fat cat's back

averaged harassed bachelor
fancy alabaster statue
classic laugh track

Distinguish Between

ɛər	ær
hairy	Harry
merry	marry
parent	apparent
Ariel	arrogance
airy	arrow
hilarious	Harold
caring	Carol

ɛər	ær
chary	charity
pair	paragraph
Karen	caramel
harem	harridan
care	character
daring	Daniel
Sarah	sanctity

Front Vowels followed by consonant "r"

The errors of Mary's arrogance
Kerry and Karen are characters
The errant airy arrow
The herald was hairy Harold
Perry's the overbearing Baron
Sherry is chary of charity
Herringbone looks hairy on Harry
The heretic harem of Harrison
The peril of the parents was apparent
Merry Mary married hairy Harry

Selections for Practice

When a merry maiden marries,
Sorrow goes and pleasure tarries;
Every sound becomes a song,
All is right, and nothing's wrong!
From today and ever after

Let our tears be tears of laughter.
Every sigh that finds a vent
Be a sigh of sweet content!
When you marry, merry maiden,
Then the air with love is laden
Chorus: Sunlight take the place of shade
When you marry, merry maid!
            The Gondoliers W. S. Gilbert

Those who play with cats must expect to be scratched.
            Miguel de Cervantes

Sometimes a troop of damsels glad,
An abbot an ambling pad
Sometimes a curly shepherd lad,
Or long-haired page in crimson clad,
Goes by to towered Camelot.
            The Lady of Shalott Alfred, Lord Tennyson

What was he doing, the great god Pan,
Down in the reeds by the river?
Spreading ruin and scattering ban,
Splashing and paddling with the hoofs of a goat,
And breaking the golden lilies afloat
With the dragon-fly on the river.
            A Musical Instrument Elizabeth Barrett Browning

The western tide crept up along the sand,
And o'er and o'er the sand,
And round and round the sand,
As far as eye could see.
The rolling mist came down and hid the land:
And never home came she.
            The Sands of Dee Charles Kingsley

…Blow, wind! come, wrack!
At least we'll die with harness on our back.
  Macbeth William Shakespeare

a

The last front vowel **a** may sound like the fifth front vowel **æ** at first, but the last front vowel **a** is sometimes called the "mid-Atlantic" vowel sound, because it's thought to be closer to the British **ɑː**. This sound is often used by American actors in classic plays for words that would take the vowel sound **ɑː** in British Standard English (R.P or Received Pronunciation) as in the word "ask." This is sometimes referred to as the "ask" list." It is also used in some of the dialects of the North of England, Scotland, and Ireland. The jaw is dropped slightly from the position of **æ**. It is not really necessary to try to distinguish between **æ** and **a** unless specifically requested to do so.

Initial

ask	aft	aunt
asking	asked	aftermath
afternoon	afterwards	after
answer	answering	afterlife

Middle

mask	demand	castle	rascal
ghastly	France	advantage	past
advance	fast	enchant	brass
paragraph	slander	calf	bath
trance	class	master	last

This sound does not occur in a final position.

Phrases for Practice

the chancellor grasped the staff   the pastor demanded a chance
the crafty last giraffe   Blanche's daft advantage
master the dance class   the last epitaph of France

Selections for Practice

Cheerily to sea! The signs of war advance
No King of England if not King of France
                    Henry V William Shakespeare

And all my days are trances,
And all my nightly dreams
 Are where thy gray eye glances
And where thy footstep gleams—
In what ethereal dances,
By what eternal streams.
                    To One in Paradise Edgar Allen Poe

There is sweet music here that softer falls
Than petals from blown roses on the grass,
Or night-dews on still waters between walls
Of shadowy granite, in a gleaming pass;
            Choric Song of the Lotus-Eaters Alfred, Lord Tennyson

Marry, this well carried shall on her behalf
Change slander to remorse;…
                    Much Ado About Nothing William Shakespeare

And when like her, Oh Saki, you shall pass
Among the guests Star-scattered on the Grass,
And in your joyous errand reach the spot
Where I made One—turn down an empty Glass!
                The Rubaiyat of Omar Khayyám Edward Fitzgerald

Now I want
Spirits to enforce, art to enchant…
                    The Tempest Shakespeare

From street to street he piped advancing,
And step for step they followed dancing,
  The Pied Piper of Hamlin Robert Browning

The Middle Vowels

3ː Key Vowel

3ː   earn

ə   a

ʌ   buck

The middle vowels have a *neutral* shape; the tip of the tongue is behind the lower front teeth and the jaw is half open. The middle of the tongue is arching forward. Don't confuse the vowel 3ː with the consonant **r** because this will cause the tip of the tongue to pull back.

3ː
Initial

earth	urban	early	earn
earl	Irma	Earnest	irk
urchin	Irving	err	ermine
urn	erred	Ursula	irksome
urge	Erlking	ergo	urgent

Medial

worm	colonel	birth	journey
worship	hearse	learn	mirth
pearl	murmur	whirl	year
serve	burl	unfurl	world
mercy	herd	virtuous	courtesy

Final

her	cur	fur	connoisseur
prefer	whir	purr	masseur
burr	sir	amateur	occur

myrrh	were	defer	spur
astir	aver	infer	were

r *Coloring*

The first and second middle vowels ɜː and ə are pronounced with the coloration of the consonant **r** before another consonant in standard American stage speech. This gives the color of the American **r** sound but doesn't restrict the voice by having the tongue pull back in the inverted or retroflex ɻ. This is shown in phonetics by the following marking ˞. This is used mainly in classic plays when the part calls for a more neutral American sound.

ɜˑ˞	err	turn	were
ə˞	father	other	lover

Practice Phrases

Ursula, shirr her skirt	the earl inferred the worse
her first words were heard	Earnest preferred amateurs
world's worst thirst	a dearth of earthworms

Selections for Practice

When I was a lad I served a term
As office boy to an attorney's firm.
I cleaned the windows and I swept the floor,
And polished up the handle of the big front door.
> *H.M.S. Pinafore* W. S. Gilbert

The barge she sat in, like a burnished throne,
Burned on the water; the poop was beaten gold;
Purple the sails, and so perfumed that
The winds were love-sick with them.
> *Antony and Cleopatra* Shakespeare

Earnest! My own Earnest! I felt from the first that you could have no other name.
> *The Importance of Being Earnest* Oscar Wilde

By the rude bridge that arched the flood,
Their flag to April's breeze unfurled,
Here once the embattled farmers stood
And fired the shot heard round the world.
      Concord Hymn Ralph Waldo Emerson

Earth-day or birth-day—
Which the true mirth-day?
Birthday or earth-day—
Which the well worth-day
      Unknown

We are not the first
Who, with best meaning, have incurr'd the worst..
      King Lear William Shakespeare

ə

The second middle vowel is called the schwa. It is always *unstressed* and is used more than any other sound in the language. The tip of the tongue is behind the lower front teeth.

The most common problem with this sound is the tendency to overstress it and substitute a stronger vowel in its place. This has the effect of double stressing a word.

Initial

about	announce	among	aghast
attention	attest	addition	alone
account	around	affront	avoid
atone	attraction	arrest	obtain
allude	above	afraid	opinion

Medial

particular	standard	tomorrow	medicine
machinery	persuade	poem	tradition

organdy	orient	orchard	method
rosary	dictionary	Texas	testimony
mayonnaise	insensible	insolent	million

Final

piper	thinker	washer	China
liar	tattler	father	dinner
familiar	finer	sinner	delta
diner	lower	planner	pizza
thinner	sister	tower	stigma

Articles and the Schwa

When the article "the" is followed by a consonant it is pronounced with the schwa **ə**. When the article is followed by a vowel it is pronounced with the short **i**

ə	iː	ə	iː
the liar	the apple	the sinner	the orange
the spade	the elephant	the crow	the owl
the crown	the earth	the sun	the arm
the book	the evening	the world	the urn
the spoon	the artist	the sea	the orb

Support him by the arm   all the world's a stage

the icy fang of winter   the most hollow lover

When the articles "an, a" are followed by a consonant or a vowel they are pronounced with the schwa **ə**

ən	ə	ən	ə
an apple	a book	an olive	a school
an event	a shame	an evening	a thought
an opening	a shirt	an orchard	a ship
an opera	a frame	an earring	a dress
an ocean	a term	an outing	a rope

Selections for Practice

…jam tomorrow and jam yesterday—but never jam today.

Through the Looking Glass Lewis Carroll

No, thy words are too precious to be cast away upon curs. Throw some of them
at me; come lame me with reasons.
    As You Like It William Shakespeare

Tomorrow and tomorrow and tomorrow, creeps in
This petty pace from day to day,
To the last syllable of recorded time;
And all our yesterday's have lighted fools
The way to dusty death. Out, out, brief candle!
    Macbeth

Now entertain conjecture of a time
When creeping murmur and the pouring dark
Fills the wide vessel of the universe.
    Henry V William Shakespeare

Hast thou, spirit,
Perform'd to point the tempest that I bade thee?
    The Tempest William Shakespeare

From camp to camp the hum of either army
Stilly sounds that the fixed sentinels
Almost receive the secret whispers of each others watch.
    Henry V William Shakespeare

All the world's a stage
And all the men and women merely players;
    As You Like It William Shakespeare

Λ

The third middle vowel **Λ** is often called the "dull vowel" because it is short and
a rather colorless It is only used in a *stressed* syllable of a word.

Initial

up	ugly	umber	unmake
umbrella	uxorious	Ulster	upstairs
onion	utter	ugly	unfit
other	undone	upper	unjust
upset	umbrage	upwards	unmask

Medial

enough	love	chunk	Russia
slough	twopence	cupboard	butter
thunder	wondrous	enough	shut
chutney	comfort	covenant	dost
comely	slovenly	borough	doth

This sound is not used at the end of a word.

Phrases for Practice

Cuthbert will cut and run	refund Tucker's lunch money
comely Russian judge	tuck up
sudden rough justice	wonderful touch of musk

Selections for Practice

There was a rustling that seem'd like a bustling
Of merry crowds justling at pitching and hustling.
> *The Pied Piper of Hamlin* Robert Browning

When the hurly burly's done,
When the battle's lost and won.
> *Macbeth* William Shakepeare

For every evil under the sun,
There is a remedy or there is none.
If there be one, seek till you find it;
If there be none, never mind it.
> *Mother Goose*

"O oysters," said the Carpenter,
You've had a pleasant run!
Shall we be trotting home again?
But answer came there none—
And this was scarcely odd, because
They'd eaten every one.
  The Walrus and the Carpenter Lewis Carroll

Then conquer we must, for our cause it is just,
And this be our motto, "In God is our trust!"
  "The Star-Spangled Banner" Francis Scott Key

Whither I must, I must; and, to conclude
This evening must I leave you, gentle Kate,
  The Taming of the Shrew William Shakespeare

The Back Vowels

uː *Key Vowel*

uː	who
ʊ	would
o	obey
ɔː	all
ɒ	honest
ɑː	artists

The lips should be *rounded* for **uː**. Suck on the end of a pencil and slowly pull it out of your mouth to find the right shape for this sound. The tip of the tongue is behind the lower front teeth and the back of the tongue is arching forward.

Initial

oodles	oozed	ooze
oolong	oomph	ourie
oozing	oozy	ooziness
oozier	ooziest	oof
oozily	oolite	ooly

Medial

cool	fruit	glued	screwed
spruce	newt	zoos	woof
doom	tool	whose	noose
soothe	rooster	choose	lose
voodoo	bloom	schooner	coupon

Final

too	few	new	blue
zoo	clue	hue	mew
do	flew	Jew	stew
sue	pew	who	goo
woo	chew	view	true

Phrases for Practice

You! Who are you?	shoot the cruel ghoul
Doom, doom, doom!	loosen the noose
too few crew	whose new blue shoes

Selections for Practice

Give me some music; music, moody food
Of us that trade in love.
> *Antony and Cleopatra* William Shakespeare

As the holly groweth green,
And never changeth hue,
So I am, ever hath been
Unto my lady true.
> *King Henry VIII* William Shakespeare

Death will come when thou art dead,
Soon, too soon—
Sleep will come when thou art fled;
Of neither would I ask the boon
I ask of thee, beloved Night—

Swift by thine approaching flight,
Come soon, soon!
        Night Percy Bysshe Shelley

And we passed through the end of the vista,
But were stopped by the door of a tomb—
By the door of a legended tomb;
And I said: what is written sweet sister,
On the door of this legended tomb?
She replied: "Ulalume—Ulalume
'Tis the vault of thy lost Ulalume!"
        Ulalume Edgar Allen Poe

The Pool Players.
Seven at the Golden Shovel
We real cool. We
Left school. We
Lurk late. We
strike straight. We
Sing sin. We
Thin gin. We
Jazz June. We
Die soon.
        We Real Cool Gwendolyn Brooks

ʊ

Keep the rounding for the first back vowel **uː** and drop your jaw for the second back vowel **ʊ**. Remember to keep it short.

This sound does not occur in an initial or final position.

Medial

| put | rook | wolf | pulpit |
| bullet | woolen | full | Worcestershire |

cushion	sugar	would	push
forsook	foot	ruin	look
Worcester	cuckoo	pull	cook

Phrases for Practice

good cook book　　　　　　Brooklyn butcher
good looking crook　　　　good sugar cookies
worsted woolen hood　　　the wolf withstood the bullet

Selections for Practice

Would not, could not, would not could not
Would not join the dance.
Would not could not, would not could not
Could not join the dance.

　　　The Lobster Quadrille Lewis Carroll

That boy with the grave mathematical look
Made believe he had written a wonderful book,
And the Royal Society thought it was true!
So they chose him right in; a good joke it was too!

　　　The Boys Oliver Wendel Holmes

The moon above the eastern wood
Shone at its full; the hill-range stood
Transfigured in the silver flood.

　　　Snowbound John Greenleaf Whittier

Like hungry guests, a sitting audience looks;
Plays are like suppers, poets are the cooks.

　　　"The Inconstant" George Farquhar

Love goes toward love, as schoolboys from their books,
But love from love, toward school with heavy looks.

　　　Romeo and Juliet William Shakespeare

o

The short vowel **o** is only used in an *unstressed* syllable. It is the first sound in the diphthong **oŭ** which is used in a *stressed* syllable. Round the lips for the first back vowel **uː** and then drop for the second back vowel **ʊ** and once again for this—the third back vowel **o**.

This sound is lengthened in Irish and Scottish dialects **oː** and is used in place of the diphthong **oŭ**.

Initial

opaque	oblique	overt
O'Neill	Ohio	omission
O'Rourke	officious	O'Toole

Medial

Bohemia	notorious	stoic
rotunda	romantic	modiste
hobo	foment	Yosemite

the notorious hobo   Odessa aroused Bohemia
vociferously opposed cocaine   O'Hara omits Ohio

Selections for Practice

Romantic Ireland's dead and gone,
It's with O'Leary in the grave.
> *September 1913* William Butler Yeats

This is the grave of Mike O'Day
Who died maintaining his right of way.
His right was clear, his will was strong,
But he's just as dead as if he'd been wrong.
> Anonymous

For the Colonel's lady and Judy O' Grady
Are sisters under their skin.
> *The Ladies* Rudyard Kipling

ɔː

Drop the jaw once more keeping the same rounding in the lips for **uː** and drop through the back vowels to the fourth back vowel **ɔː**. You should be able to insert two fingers into your mouth with your lips rounded.

Initial

all	auto	audience	awkward
auction	awful	autumn	altar
almost	already	August	austere
orb	awning	awe	awl
always	auspices	auto	author

Medial

Paul	caught	lawyer	yawn
scald	slaughter	broad	decorum
laundry	lawn	tall	faucet
drawn	Saul	taunt	warrior
talk	gaunt	sauce	hoarse

Final

paw	saw	thaw	braw
gnaw	Shaw	slaw	McGraw
haw	law	raw	Waugh
withdraw	jaw	claw	draw
flaw	straw	craw	maw

Phrases for Practice

the audacity of Aubrey's lawyer

Auden, Maughm and Waugh are all authors

Austin and Albany were caught

all applauded automatically

Paul thought Shaw was the author

slaughter of Cawdor

authors are all talk

extraordinary decorum

Saul applauded Laura

autumnal dawn

Selections for Practice

The wrinkled sea beneath him crawls,
 He watches from his mountain walls,
And like a thunderbolt he falls.
            The Eagle Alfred, Lord Tennyson

I am all the daughters of my father's house,
And all the brothers too;—and yet I know not.
            Twelfth Night Shakespeare

All knowing
All powerful
Lord of the Dawn, we hail Thee
All seeing
All merciful
Lord of the Night we call on Thee.
            Anonymous

"In my youth," said his father, "I took to the law,
And argued each case with my wife;
And the muscular strength which it gave to my jaw
Has lasted the rest of my life."
            Alice in Wonderland Lewis Carroll

I know not whether Laws be right,
Or whether Laws be wrong;
All that we know who lie in gaol
Is that the wall is strong;
And that each day is like a year,
A year whose days are long
            The Ballad of Reading Gaol Oscar Wilde

Rough wind, that moanest loud
Grief too sad for song;

Wild wind, when sullied cloud
Knells all the night long
Sad storm, whose tears are vain.
Bare woods whose branches strain,
Deep caves and dreary main
Wail, for the world's wrong
          "A Dirge" Percy Bysshe Shelley

I am the daughter of earth and water,
And the nursling of the sky;
I pass through the pores of the ocean and shores;
I change, but I cannot die.
          The Cloud Percy Bysshe Shelley

ɒ

Drop the jaw from the position of the fourth back vowel ɔː, keeping the lips slightly rounded. The vowel ɒ is short and crisp and is often confused with the fourth back vowel ɔː, and the last back vowel ɑː. It is used in standard stage speech and for British Received Pronunciation.

Initial

opportunity	honor	oxen	Osmond
honest	office	offered	ox
ominous	orange	odd	octopus
often	occident	off	oscillate
offing	opera	olive	Oscar

Medial

coffee	gone	foreign	borrow
chorus	bomb	monster	popular
toffee	wash	song	horror
Tom	common	hobby	stopped
cough	pot	lost	wanted

This sound does not occur in a final position.

Phrases for Practice

Bob's modern yacht	copper coffee pot
a box of hot chocolate	ominous occidental bomb
popular foreign correspondent	snobbish jockey
Tom's common hobby	odd orange frog
strong honest coffee	intoxicated Scots mob

Distinguish between the last three back vowels: ɔː ɒ ɑː

Paul wants calm.	Father is fond of drama.
Magdalen College is in Oxford.	Massage the monster's paw.
Tomorrow is all calm.	The horrible harlot stopped Paul.
The sponsor talked to father.	The call was harmless.

Selections for Practice

To sit in solemn silence in a dull, dark dock,
In a pestilential prison, with a life-long lock,
Awaiting the sensation of a short, sharp shock,—
From a cheap and chippy chopper on a big, black block.
　　The Mikado W. S. Gilbert

A garden is a lovesome thing, God wot!
Rose plot,
Fringed pool,
Ferned grot,
The veriest school
Of peace; and yet the fool
Contends that God is not—
Not God! In gardens! when the eve is cool?
Nay, but I have a sign;
'Tis very sure God walks in mine.
　　　T. E. Brown

If a Hottentot tot taught a Hottentot tot
To talk e'er the tot could totter,
Ought the Hottentot tot be taught to say aught,
Or what ought to be taught her?
        Edward Lear

We look before and after,
 And pine for what is not:
Our sincerest laughter
 With some pain is fraught;
Our sweetest songs are those that tell of saddest thought.
        To a Skylark Percy Bysshe Shelley

There was a little girl who had a little curl,
Right in the middle of her forehead,
When she was good, she was very, very good,
And when she was bad she was horrid.
        William Wadsworth Longfellow

ɑː

Let the jaw drop with the lips slightly rounded and the back of the tongue relaxed and forward with the tip of the tongue behind the lower front teeth.

Initial

alms	aria	almond
artist	ark	argue
armistice	arbor	arms
art	armor	ardor
arch	arcade	Arctic

Medial

Harvard	scar	
carcass	sergeant	tarnish
psalm	cart	hardy

cardinal	garment	harvest
marble	harm	parsley

Final

bar	par	mar
far	tar	cigar
char	star	car
jar	disbar	gar

Phrases for Practice

calm the sergeant	harness the farm cart
large barn yard	the art of the aria
far harbor	ask Father to pardon Carl

Selections for Practice

There are maidens in Scotland more lovely by far,
That would gladly be bride to young Lochinvar.
> *Lochinvar* Sir Walter Scott

When I, good friends, was called to the bar,
I'd an appetite fresh and hearty,
But I was, as many young barristers are,
An impecunious party.
> *Trial by Jury* W. S. Gilbert

I engage with the Snark—every night after dark—
in a dreamy delirious fight;
I serve it with greens in those shadowy scenes,
And I use it for striking a light.——
> *The Hunting of the Snark* Lewis Carroll

Sunset and evening star,
And one clear call for me,
And may there be no moaning of the bar

When I put out to sea.
Twilight and evening bell,
And after that the dark
And may there be no sadness of farewell,
When I embark.
For though from out our bourne of Time and Place
The flood may bear me far,
I hope to see my Pilot face to face,
When I have crossed the bar.

Crossing the Bar Alfred, Lord Tennyson

It is the lark that sings so out of tune,
Straining harsh discords and unpleasing sharps

Romeo and Juliet William Shakespeare

My soul is dark—Oh! Quickly string
The harp I yet can brook to hear;
And let thy gentle fingers fling
Its melting murmurs o'er mine ear.

My Soul Is Dark Lord Byron

Of all the girls that are so smart
There's none like pretty Sally;
She is the darling of my heart,
And she lives in our alley.

Sally in Our Alley Henry Carey

The English Diphthongs

eĭ   aĭ   ɔĭ   oŭ   ɑŭ
ıə̆   ɛə̆   ʊə̆   ɔə̆   ɑə̆

Diphthongs are combinations of two vowel sounds blended together to form one sound. The first element is always stronger than the second and this is shown in phonetics by the unstressed mark ˘. There are ten diphthongs in spoken English.

The first five diphthongs, **eĭ aĭ ɔĭ oŭ aŭ**, may be long or short depending on what follows them.

The last five diphthongs, **ĭɚ ɛɚ ŭɚ ɔɚ aɚ**, are called the diphthongs of R because the letter R is at the end of the word.

The first five diphthongs, **eĭ aĭ ɔĭ oŭ aŭ**, are fully long in a stressed syllable before a pause:

> lay, reply, annoy, grow, vow

or followed by one or more *voiced* consonants in the same syllable and the diphthong appears in the *last* syllable:

> laid, replied, annoyed, grows, vowel

An exception to this rule occurs when the voiced consonant following the diphthong is itself followed by one or more voiceless consonants:

> paints, pints, points, pounce

The diphthongs are short when followed by a voiceless consonant:

> fate, hike, oyster, boat, out

or when they occur in the first syllable of words of two or more syllables:

> fading, hiking, oiling, boatmen, outing

This may seem overly complicated and it is fair to say that most native speakers of English have no difficulty with the length of vowels and diphthongs. However, it does not hurt to understand some of the properties of the length of vowel and diphthong sounds. For a student whose principal language is not English these rules can be especially helpful in avoiding over pronouncing words.

eĭ

The diphthong **eĭ** is a combination of the third front vowel **e** and the second front vowel **ɪ**. The two are blended together to form one sound. Don't let the jaw drop too far down for this sound—let it drop only as far as the third front vowel **e**.

Initial

aim	ale	age	ague
ape	able	aviary	amiable

ache	aitch	ace	aviator
ate	acorn	apiary	aviation
Amos	Amy	amen	alien

Medial

bayberry	sage	bake	nape
bathe	way	made	waif
shake	pale	amaze	maimed
shame	weighed	mace	weighed
station	halfpenny	vacate	shale

Final

may	shay	dray	fey
lay	nay	stray	replay
bray	ray	hay	bay
way	whey	fray	stay
display	inveigh	portray	day

Phrases for Practice

ape's fake grimace	narrate an amazing tale
Drake sailed away	they ate eight acorns
create day by day	amiable vague face
bake eight date cakes	late railway train

Selections for Practice

Come dear children, let us away;
Down and away below!
Now my brothers call from the bay,
Now the great winds shoreward blow,
Now the salt tides seaward flow;
Now the wild white horses play,
Champ and chafe and toss in the spray.
Children dear, let us away!
This way, this way!

   The Forsaken Merman Matthew Arnold

Boot, saddle, to horse and away!
Rescue my castle before the hot day
Brightens to blue from its silvery gray.
(Chorus)—Boot, saddle, to horse, and away!
      Robert Browning

I wield the flail of the lashing hail,
And whiten the green plains under,
And then again I dissolve it in rain,
And laugh as I pass in thunder.
      The Cloud Percy Bysshe Shelley

Said the little Eohippus,
"I am going to be a horse!
And on my middle finger-nails
To run my earthly course;
I'm going to have a flowing tail!
I'm going to have a mane!
I'm going to stand fourteen hands high
On the psychozoic plain.
      Similar Cases Charlotte Perkins Gilman

By the margin, willow veiled,
Slide the heavy barges trailed
By slow horses; and unhailed
The shallop flitteth silken-sailed
Skimming down to Camelot.
      The Lady of Shalott Alfred, Lord Tennyson

Time, you old gipsy man,
Will you not stay,
Put up your caravan
Just for one day?
      Time You Old Gipsy Man Ralph Hodgson

aɪ

The diphthong **aɪ** is a combination of the last front vowel **a** and the second front vowel **ɪ**. Since they are both front vowels, the lips are slightly spread. The jaw drops down for **a** and then immediately comes up for **ɪ** blending the two sounds.

Initial

I	aisle	ice	Ike
I'm	ivy	eyes	icicle
I'll	I'd	item	aisle
eyelid	icon	irony	Eiffel
ivory	iron	identity	itemize

Medial

tribe	pied	geyser	climb
Michael	dynasty	knife	guile
height	vice	stripe	smiled
pike	direst	prizes	rhyme
pyres	inquiry	advertise	died

Final

fie	try	nigh	buy
dry	reply	defy	pie
why	Guy	thigh	my
shy	rye	deny	vie
rely	sty	high	apply

Phrases for Practice

Irish dynasty	Michael beguiled Ivy
the shy child	Time revived Iceland
light the pyre	the tribe revived the Nile

Selections for Practice

If a hart do lack a hind
Let him seek out Rosalind

If the cat will after kind,
So be sure will Rosalind
Winter'd garments must be lined,
So must slender Rosalind,
They that reap must sheaf and bind,
Then to cart with Rosalind,
Sweetest nut hath sourest rind,
Such a nut is Rosalind,
He that sweetest rose will find,
Must find love's prick, and Rosalind.
　　　　As You Like It　William Shakespeare

Where the sea snakes coil and twine,
Dry their mail and bask in the brine;
Where great whales come sailing by,
Sail and sail with unshut eye,
Round the world forever and aye.
　　　　The Forsaken Merman　Matthew Arnold

Little Fly,
Thy summer's play
My thoughtless hand
Has brushed away.
Am not I
A fly like thee?
Or art not thou
A man like me?
For I dance
And drink and sing,
'Till some blind hand
Shall brush my wing.
If thought is life
And strength and breath,
And the want of thought is death,

Then am I
A happy fly
If I live
Or if I die.
        The Fly William Blake

ɔɪ̆

The diphthong **ɔɪ̆** is a combination of the fourth back vowel **ɔː** and the second
front vowel **ɪ**. The shape of the sound blends the rounding of the back vowel **ɔː**
with the slightly spread shape of the front vowel **ɪ**.

Initial

oil	oily	oil can
ointment	oilcloth	oyster
oink	oint	oil well
oilskin	oilstone	oiliest
oiled	oiler	oilfield

Medial

foibles	royal	pointed	poignant
doily	noisome	hoyden	void
foyer	hoist	poison	cloister
jointure	joyful	buoyancy	employed
loyal	coinage	annoying	cloyed

Final

annoy	destroy	deploy	cloy
convoy	boy	buoy	Troy
ahoy	toy	employ	Savoy
enjoy	coy	soy	goy
decoy	joy	alloy	viceroy

Phrases for Practice

joyful hoyden   destroyed Joyce's foyer

poignant voyage	noisome boiling poison
joining voices	poised royal loyalists
she's hoity-toity	enjoy the hoi polloi

Selections for Practice

The violence of either grief or joy
Their own enactures with themselves destroy;
When joy most revels, grief doth most lament;
Grief joys, joy grieves on slender accidents.
     Hamlet William Shakespeare

Here come more voices.
Your voices; for your voices I have fought:
Watched for your voices; for your voices bear
Of wounds, two dozen odd; battles thrice six
I have seen, and heard of; for your voices have
Done many things, some less, some more; your voices;
Indeed I would be consul.
     Coriolanus William Shakespeare

Then sweet the hour that brings release from labor and from toil;
We talk the battle over and share the battle's spoil.
     The Battle Field William Cullen Bryant

The devil hath not, in all his quiver's choice,
An arrow for the heart like a sweet voice.
     Don Juan Lord Byron

There was a Young Lady of Troy
Whom several large flies did annoy;
Some she killed with a thump, some she drowned at the pump,
And some she took with her to Troy.
     A Book of Nonsense Edward Lear

oŭ

The diphthong **oŭ** is a combination of the third back vowel **o** and the second back vowel **ʊ**. The lips are very rounded.

Initial

oh	ode	old	open
okra	oak	omen	oakum
oaf	ochre	olden	oath
only	oats	owe	obi
oldest	own	oatmeal	oaken

Medial

home	gloat	coterie	remote
most	poetry	goad	trophy
rogue	zone	disclosed	jovial
stoke	roam	vogue	loaves
loathe	known	alone	crony

Final

mow	bow	hoe	Poe
stow	low	snow	bow
show	foe	apropos	slow
go	though	no	grow
woe	row	dough	flow

Phrases for Practice

provoking toad	gloating coterie
Poe's copious poetry	doleful smoke
loathed associate	oldest brooch

Selections for Practice

Gold, gold, gold, gold,
Bright and yellow, hard and cold
Molten, graven, hammered, and rolled

Heavy to get and hard to hold,
Hoarded, bartered, bought and sold,
Stolen, borrowed, squandered, doled:
Spurned by the young, but hugged by the old
To the very verge of the church yard mold,
Gold, gold, gold, gold.
    Gold Thomas Hood

Toad that under cold stone
Days and nights has thirty-one...
    Macbeth William Shakespeare

In Flanders fields the poppies blow
Between the crosses, row on row,
That mark our place; and in the sky
The larks, still bravely singing fly,
Scarce heard amidst the guns below.
    In Flanders Field John D. McCrae

Oh, western wind, when wilt thou blow
The small rain down, can rain?
Christ if my love were in my arms.
And I in my bed again.
    Unknown Poet 15th Century

Sweet and low, sweet and low,
Wind of the western sea,
Low, low breathe and blow,
Wind of the western sea!
Over the rolling waters go,
Come from the dying moon, and blow,
Blow him again to me;
While my little one, while my pretty one, sleeps.
    "The Princess" Alfred, Lord Tennyson

aʊ

The diphthong **aʊ** is a combination of the last back vowel **a:** and the second back vowel **ʊ**. Keep the rounding in the lips with the soft palate high.

Initial

owl	out	ouster	outdoors
ounce	hour	ouch	outboard
ourselves	outing	outside	outdo
hourly	ours	hourglass	outage
outlay	outfit	outlaw	outcast

Medial

wound	mouth	scowling	carouse
grouse	dowager	vowel	clout
trowel	shower	scour	powder
dowry	cloud	devouring	douse
pounce	lout	mountain	clown

Final

slough	bow	sow	avow
pow	now	how	chow
cow	bough	allow	plough
vow	thou	endow	brow
row	wow	prow	scow

Phrases for Practice

how now brown cow	plow the surrounding ground
prowled the scow	endow the count with the crown
allow the pow wow	vowed our dowry
outmoded brown gown	outlying towns
outnumbered outposts	outrageous outlaw

Selections for Practice

The owl looked down with his great round eyes
At the lowering clouds and the darkening skies,

"A good night for scouting," says he.
"A mouse or two may be found on the ground
Or a fat little bird in a tree."
So down he flies from the old church tower,
The mouse and the birdie crouch and cower,
Back he flies in half an hour,
"A very good supper," says he.
       Anonymous

Round about Titania's bower,
Strange clouds of fairy flowers are found.
      A Midsummer Night's Dream Shakespeare

Come, thou monarch of the vine,
Plumpy Bacchus with pink eyne!
In thy vats our cares be drown'd
With thy grapes our hairs be crown'd.
Cup us, till the world go round,
Cup us, till the world go round!
      Antony and Cleopatra William Shakespeare

Now is the winter of our discontent
Made glorious summer by the sun of York;
And all the clouds that lour'd upon our house
In the deep bosom of the ocean buried.
Now are our brows bound with victorious wreaths;
Our bruised arms hung up for monuments;
Our stern alarums changed to merry meetings;
Our dreadful marches to delightful measures.
      Richard III William Shakespeare

Down, down I come, like glist'ring Phaeton,
Wanting the manage of unruly jades.
      Richard II William Shakespeare

Take this kiss upon the brow!
And, in parting from you now,
Thus much let me avow:
You are not wrong, who deem
That my days have been a dream;
　　　A Dream Within a Dream   Edgar Allan Poe

The Short Diphthongs of R

ɪɚ̆   ɛɚ̆   ʊɚ̆   ɔɚ̆   ɑɚ̆

The diphthongs ɪɚ̆ ɛɚ̆ ʊɚ̆ ɔɚ̆ ɑɚ̆ are called the diphthongs of **R** because the letter **R** is in the spelling at the end of the syllable in which the sound occurs. However, the actual sound used is the *schwa*. If the word that follows begins with a consonant, the schwa can be given a slight R coloration.

　　ɪɚ̆˞

　　fear fire

If the following word begins with a vowel, the R is linked into the vowel.

　　ɛɚ̆r

　　pair of

ɪɚ̆	ɛɚ̆	ʊɚ̆	ɔɚ̆	ɑɚ̆
peer	pair	poor	pour	par
fear	fair	fewer	for	far
beer	bare	boor	bore	bar
mere	Mary	moor	more	mar
deer	dare	dour	door	dark
cheer	charity	chewier	chore	char

Diphthong of R Combinations for Practice

peer power	dark beer	mature charm
careful charity	fair Mary	curious shark
fewer bores	lurid theater	airy moor
cheerful poor	boring chore	pour tar

Selections for Practice

Who is this? And what is here?
And in the lighted palace near
Died the sound of royal cheer;
And they crossed themselves for fear,
All the knights at Camelot.
The Lady of Shalott Alfred, Lord Tennyson

But know I think, and think I know most sure,
My art is not past power, nor you past cure.
All's Well That Ends Well William Shakespeare

Enough! No more!
It is not so sweet now as it was before
Twelfth Night William Shakespeare

That with music loud and long,
I would build that dome in air,
That sunny dome; those caves of ice;
And all who hear should see them there,
And all should cry, Beware! Beware!
His flashing eyes, his floating hair!
Kubla Khan Samuel Taylor Coleridge

Tommy's tears and Mary's fears
Will make them old before their years.
Mother Goose

Here, Oh hear:
We bear the bier
Of the Father of many a canceled year!
Prometheus Unbound Percy Bysshe Shelley

Sigh no more ladies, sigh no more,
Men were deceivers ever,
One foot on sea and one on shore,
To one thing constant never.

       Much Ado About Nothing William Shakespeare

Your badinage so airy,
Your manner arbitrary,
Are out of place
When face to face
With an influential fairy.
We never knew we were speaking to
An influential fairy.

       Iolanthe W. S. Gilbert

The owl looked up to the stars above
 And sang to a small guitar
"O lovely Pussy! O Pussy, my love,
What a beautiful Pussy you are,
You are,
You are!
What a beautiful Pussy you are!"

       The Owl and the Pussy-Cat Edward Lear

The Triphthongs

aɪɜ̆   ɑʊɜ̆

A triphthong is a sound in which three vowel sounds are blended to form one sound. There are two triphthongs in spoken English all ending in R.

aɪɜ̆	ɑʊɜ̆
ire	our
pyre	power
byre	bower
fire	flower

tire	tower
dire	dower
lyre	lower
shire	shower
fire power	our ire
dire tower	flowery byre
briar bower	shower higher

Selections for Practice

Fire, fire, fire, fire!
Tell the boys who're in the choir
The flames are leaping higher and higher.
Run and find the village squire,
The fire's spreading higher and higher.

      Anonymous

Glendower left his tower on the heights
And summoned all the power of his knights.
He rode down with aspect sour
To make his subjects cower,
But they glowered at Glendower and his knights.

      Anonymous

Above the lowly plants it towers,
The fennel with its yellow flowers.
And, in an earlier age than ours,
Was gifted with the wondrous powers
Long vision to restore.

      The Goblet of Life William Wadsworth Longfellow

Fate all flowery,
Bright and bowery
Is her dowry!

      The Yeoman of the Guard W. S. Gilbert

Like a high-born maiden
In a palace tower,
Soothing her love-laden
Soul in secret hour
With music sweet as love, which overflows her bower:
> *To a Skylark* Percy Bysshe Shelley

I am a woodland fellow, sir, that always loved a great fire;
And the master I speak of ever keeps a good fire.
> *All's Well That Ends Well* William Shakespeare

Tongue Twisters for Practice

I'm not the pheasant plucker, I'm the pheasant plucker's mate
And I'm only plucking pheasants 'cause the pheasant plucker's late.

If a Hottentot tot taught a Hottentot tot
To talk e'er the tot could totter
Ought the Hottentot tot be taught to say aught
Or what ought to be taught her?
> Edward Lear

A tutor who tooted the flute
Tried to tutor two tutors to toot;
Said the two to the tutor,
"Is it harder to toot, or to tutor two tutors to toot?"

The Leith police dismisseth us.

Amidst the mists and coldest frosts
With stoutest wrists and loudest boasts
He thrusts his fists against the posts,
And still insists he sees the ghosts.

Zinty, Tinty, tuppenny bun
The cock went out to have some fun.

He had some fun, he beat the drum,
Zinty Tinty, tuppenny Bun

Peter Prangle, the prickly, prangly pear picker
picked a peck of prickly, prangly pears
from the prickly, prangly pear trees on the pleasant prairies.

Betty Botta bought some butter
But, said she, this. butter's bitter,
If I put it in my batter,
It will make my batter bitter.
But a bit of better butter,
Will make my bitter batter better..
So she bought a bit of butter.
Better than the bitter butter,
And it made her bitter batter better.
So 'twas better Betty Botta bought
A bit of better butter.

Theophilus Thistle, the successful thistle sifter, in sifting a sieve full of unsifted thistles, thrust three thousand thistles through the thick of his thumb. Now if Theophilus Thistle the successful thistle sifter, in sifting a sieve full of unsifted thistles, thrust three thousand thistles through the thick of his thumb, see that thou in sifting a sieve full of unsifted thistles thrust not three thousand thistles through the thick of thy thumb. Success to the successful thistle sifter.

All I want is a proper cup of coffee
Made in a proper copper coffee pot.
I may be off my dot—
But I want a cup of coffee
From a proper coffee pot.
Tin coffee pots or iron coffee pots,
They're no use to me.
If I can't have a proper cup of coffee

In a proper copper coffee pot
I'll have a cup of tea.

Whether the weather be fine,
Or whether the weather be not,
Whether the weather be cold,
Or whether the weather be hot,
We'll weather the weather,
Whatever the weather,
Whether we like it or not.
Robert Rowley rolled a round roll round,
Where rolled the round roll
Robert Rowley rolled round?

Sheila's Shetland pony shied
Shooting Sheila on the shore.
Shaking Sheila, stupefied,
Struggled homeward stiff and sore.

What a todo to die today
At a minute or two to two,
A thing distinctly hard to say
And harder still to do,
For they'll beat a tattoo at a quarter to two
A rat-a-tat-tat-a-tat-at two
And the dragon will come when he hears the drum,
At a minute or two to two today,
At a minute or two to two.

Round and round the great arena,
Roared the Roman charioteers.

Rubber baby buggy bumpers.

Algy met a bear.
The bear was bulgy, and the bulge was Algy.

A tree toad loved a she-toad
Who lived up in a tree.
He was a two-toed tree toad
But a three-toed toad was she.
The two-toed tree toad tried to win
The three-toed she-toad's heart
For the two-toed tree toad loved the ground
That the three-toed tree toad trod.
But the two-toed tree toad tried in vain.
He couldn't please her whim
From her tree toad bower
With her three-toed power.

The road to Rome is rugged, rough and round.

I rattled my bottles in Rollock's yard

Sister Suzie's sewing shirts for soldiers
Such skill at sewing shirts our shy young sister Susie Shows!
The soldiers sent epistles, saying they'd sooner sleep on thistles,
Than the saucy, soft short shirts for soldiers Sister Suzie sews.

The English International Phonetic Alphabet

The English Vowels and Diphthongs

Vowels

Front

iː	he
ɪ	will
e	let
æ	Ann
a	pass

Middle

ɜː	earn
ə	a
ʌ	buck

Back

uː	who
ʊ	would
o	obey
ɔː	all
ɒ	honest
ɑː	fathers

Diphthongs

eĭ	may
aĭ	my
ɔĭ	boy
oŭ	go
aŭ	now
ɪə̆	peer
ɛə̆	pair

ʊɝ   poor
ɔɝ   pour
ɑɝ   par

The Consonants

p   pea
b   be
t   to
d   do
k   key
g   go
m   me
n   no
ŋ   hang
f   fee
v   vow
θ   thigh
ð   thy
s   so
z   zoo
ʃ   shy
ʒ   azure
r   row
h   he
tʃ   chew
dʒ   joy
ʍ   why
w   we
j   you

Chapter VI
Special Speech Problems

And speaking thick, which nature made his blemish
Became the accents of the valiant;

Henry IV, Part 2 *William Shakespeare*

There are some specific speech problems that need to be addressed before they get in the way of the actor's ability to find work and become a liability. A strong regional dialect, a whistling sibilant s, a lisp, nasality and denasality, or a tense, rigid jaw, can limit the kinds of roles for which an actor is considered and interfere with development of his or her career. The speech problems outlined in this chapter can be eliminated or greatly reduced with practice and application in your daily life. If your speech problems are the result of a physical dysfunction rather than an ingrained habit, you should consult an otolaryngologist who can make the proper diagnosis and recommend a licensed speech therapist. If you are unsure whether any of the problems identified in this chapter pertain to you, ask a theater voice and speech teacher, a director, an agent or someone competent to judge professional voices, to listen to you read and to give you their opinion.

Regional Dialects

One of the most controversial aspects of speech training for actors over the years has been the subject of the elimination of regional accents. It is controversial precisely because it deals with one of the most personal and idiosyncratic things about us as individuals—the way we sound to ourselves and those closest to us. It is part of the way we feel about ourselves, about who we are, where we come from and our sense of personal identity. When we change the way we sound to ourselves and to the world around us, we also change who we are in a very profound way.

In George Bernard Shaw's *Pygmalion*, Eliza Doolittle, the Cockney flower girl who learns to be a lady by changing her speech, describes her inability to return to her old way of speaking.

> *I can't. I could have done it once, but now I can't go back to it. Last night, when I was wandering about, a girl spoke to me; and I tried to get back into the old way with her; but it was no use. You told me, you know, that when a child is brought to a foreign country, it picks up the language in a few weeks and forgets its own. Well, I am a child in your country. I have forgotten my own language, and can speak nothing but yours.*

This poignant speech illustrates some of the fears expressed by actors or anyone attempting to change their speech. These fear need to be addressed frankly and sympathetically.

"But I won't sound like me!" is a familiar refrain in almost every beginning voice and speech class. American acting students tend to think that they are alone in their fears, believing that their British counterparts eagerly embrace pear shaped tones and speak with perfect diction.

A few years ago I was a visiting voice teacher on the Acting Course at Central School of Speech and Drama in London. Because I was replacing the regular voice teacher who was on sabbatical, I taught all the voice and speech classes, working directly with students who came from all over the British isles and from a wide background socially. The number of regional dialects the students spoke were far more extensive than anything I had ever encountered in an American drama school and, quite frankly, I was astonished at the emotional reaction some of the students had to learning Standard English, which in Britain is called R. P. or Received Pronunciation. Many of them connected R. P. to class repression and would only learn it as a second dialect to be used in performance while others, who had been brought up to speak R. P., adopted a "working class" accent to fit in. For some of them this solution of using R.P. only in performance worked very well, for others their dialect ultimately limited them to parts requiring their regional dialect.

Before we go into the details about *how* to go about losing a regional dialect, we should first explore what regional dialects means in the first place and *why* we should or shouldn't go about losing our own.

What are Regional Dialects?

Those of us from English speaking countries throughout the world share a common linguistic heritage. While an Australian speaks English with a dialect that is different from an American, an Irishman, a West Indian, or a Scot, the root language originated in the British Isles. A dialect is based on the speech of those who first colonized that country, the languages of those who followed, as well as the language of those who were there originally.

In America, the "New York" accent is a composite of many languages—Yiddish, Italian, Russian, German, Irish, Spanish and others. As the emigrant children learned to speak English, the language of their new country, they still shaped the sounds of English with the vowel and consonant shapes of their parent's language. Although they no longer had the easily recognized "foreign" accent of their parents, their speech was strongly influenced by the old language and they, in turn, passed that sound on to their children.

Australia is an interesting linguistic study. During the 18th and 19th centuries, Great Britain used it as a penal colony for the poorest of her subjects, the majority of whom spoke with a Cockney dialect. The second group most frequently sent were the Irish and the influence of those two dialects can still be heard in Australian speech to this day.

The English spoken in Ireland, especially in the western part of the island, is perhaps the oldest remnant of English as it was spoken centuries ago. Along with the lilt, one of its most striking characteristics is the strong use of the consonant "r" sound in words such as form, heart, star, roar, and warm. The strong use of the consonant r is also characteristic of Scots and the dialect in Devonshire where many of the first American colonists came from. It serves to remind us that the r sound in American English is much closer to the English spoken in Shakespeare's time than is the current British standard, R.P.

The musical and lilting cadence in the sounds of English spoken in Trinidad and much of the West Indies has the strong rhythm and flavor of African languages as well as the influence of the English spoken by many former indentured servants originally brought there from India.

Given all these different dialects from all these different English speaking countries, what, if anything, should an American acting student do about his or her own regional dialect. Is there a standard of American English for the stage or for film and television?

There is a Greek proverb which states "as the life is, so is the speech." For the actor, whose life is dedicated to portraying a variety of characters in a wide variety of plays, flexibility in speech is the key. Actors must sound like the characters they are playing, whether it is a Chicago real estate salesman in *Glengarry Glen Ross,* a Southern matron in *Steel Magnolias,* a young New York Jewish soldier in *Biloxi Blues*, or the Prince of Denmark in *Hamlet*. The language of the characters in the play determines the kind of speech required for the part.

The great Russian director Constantin Stanislavski, in his book *Building a Character*, has the following things to say about what an actor must be aware of with regard to his speech:

> *It is absolutely necessary to be made aware of the deficiencies in your speech so that you can break yourselves permanently of the habit, widespread among actors, of giving their own incorrect everyday speech as an excuse for the slovenly ways of speaking on the stage.*

The best choice for an actor, I believe, is speech that is neutral and reflects the prevailing standard of speech of his country. If the part calls for a dialect, it should be as accurate as he can make it and reflect the intention of the playwright. He should be able to be heard with ease by every member of the audience with the focus being on *what* is being said rather than *how* he or she is saying it. Actors in the theater today need to be vocally flexible; they should be able to handle the vocal demands of a variety of plays and playwrights from the classical to the contemporary.

The first performances of *Glengarry Glen Ross* by David Mamet and *Angels in America* by Tony Kushner were at The Royal National Theatre in London (not in America). English actors played the parts with American accents as they do in all American plays. As theater becomes more internationally based, American actors must become more flexible with the language of plays that differ from their own.

Standard Stage Speech

Standard Stage Speech is a rather ambiguous term. If we were somehow transported back in time about sixty or seventy years or so, we would be astonished at the voices of the actors on the stage. They would probably sound affected, artificial, and very English to our ears. That is because the stage standard at that time was English stage standard or a close approximation of it. We can even hear it in the voices of the American film actors of the period.

With the advent of The Group Theatre in the 1930s, which produced plays of social realism by playwrights such as Clifford Odets, William Saroyan, Sidney Kingsley, and Irwin Shaw, stage speech began to reflect the language of the ordinary people depicted in these plays. It was only with the rise of The Actor's Studio under the direction of Lee Strasberg, whose work emphasized the inner emotional life of the character over the external representation of that character, that the "mumbling method actor" became a caricature.

Today Standard American Stage Speech is basically unaccented American English. Actors today must have in addition the flexibility to adopt the speech sounds and rhythms inherent in a wide variety of text, whether it is a Southern lawyer in (*Crimes of the Heart*), a Boston Brahmin (*Painting Churches*), a New York Jewish grandmother (*Lost In Yonkers*), a British housewife from Liverpool (*Shirley Valentine*) or a South African schoolboy (*My Children! My Africa!*). If the play is by George Bernard Shaw (*Major Barbara*), Oscar Wilde (*An Ideal Husband*), Harold Pinter (*The Homecoming*), or Brian Friel (*Dancing at Lughnasa*), then the actor should be able to find the voice of those characters as well, whether R. P., Cockney, or Northern Irish. An actor who can handle the language of the text of plays as dissimilar as *Pericles, Les Liaisons Dangereuses, You Never Can Tell, A Streetcar Named Desire, Steel Magnolias, On the Verge, The Sea*, and *The Road To Mecca* will find that his or her employment opportunities increase. In fact the plays just mentioned were part of the season at a large regional theater where I was the company vocal coach for two seasons.

British and American Actors Approach to Regional Dialects

One of the interesting differences between working with British actors and American actors is that one of the first questions a British actor will ask is: "what is the accent like?" American actors, on the other hand, seem more preoccupied with how the character feels rather than how the character sounds. Both are important, but the outward manifestation of the inner life of the character through the way he speaks is part of the process of creating a character. In Britain, the attitude toward class and geographical differences is quite strong. Although Manchester, Liverpool, Newcastle and London are, by American standards, not very far apart, the accents are quite different. Class differences, as manifested in the regional dialect, whether it is Cockney, Geordie, Essex or R.P. are important distinctions of character for British audiences.

Losing a Regional Accent

When I was in drama school at Carnegie Tech (now Carnegie Mellon), all the students were required to lose their regional accents. Having grown up in Louisiana, I found "Southernisms" scrawled across all my speeches by Edith Skinner, my voice and speech teacher, and soon found myself in the position of having to lose an accent that outside of the theater was part of my identity. It was understood, however, that we were training for a career in the professional theater and that was part of what was expected of us in professional training. Today, I do not have a trace of a southern accent except on the stage when needed, but I do sympathize with the conflicting emotions generated by losing a regional accent.

Today, while I believe that it is possible to maintain one's regional accent, while adopting Standard Stage for certain parts, I will not pretend that it is easy. For one thing agents, casting directors and directors may not be able to get beyond your regionalism or accept that you can change your speech to suit the role. Recently I attended a conference in which a casting director for a large Shakespeare company was asked if he could overlook a regional dialect when he auditioned the actor. He said it would be very hard: "There are so many actors who *can* do it, why should I take a chance on someone that I have doubts about?" It comes down to employability. The more vocal skills you have—whether it's the ability to handle styles in a wide variety of textual material, a facility with dialects, excellent voice and diction, or a trained singing voice—will all increase your chances in a very overcrowded and highly competitive profession.

Finally, you should bear in mind that it takes time, both physically and psychically. Learning to reshape sounds in the mouth and to use the tongue differently on some sounds takes practice. It also takes time to get used to the way the new sounds feel as well as the new way you may hear yourself. The most important thing to remember is to always practice on text that is not close to your own regional accent. If you are a southerner, don't work on scenes by Tennessee Williams, Beth Henley, or Eudora Welty for a while. Find the text that allows you to *transform*—to become another character, not just yourself. Try to get the feel of the placement of the voice—you will find that there are subtle shifts in some accents. Try to feel the vibration on the voiced consonants in the mask of the face and on your lips and tongue. Remember that your ear is usually not the best guide, let the sensation of the sound, guide you as well.

Recording Devices

Some actors find a recording device very helpful in allowing them to monitor the sound of their voice, while others find it discouraging. If you are upset when you hear the sound of your own voice on a tape recorder, work without it, until you feel more confident.

Family and Friends

One word of caution about the reactions of friends and family to your new speech: you may find their reactions discouraging because they may not want you to change. They may find your new voice threatening to their relationship with you. They may regard your new speech sounds as a rejection of them. It is important to remember that this is a normal reaction and to try not to let it bother you. Remember that real friends will understand that what you are doing is necessary for you to enhance your range of skills to obtain work as a professional actor.

Characteristic of American Regionalisms

The following regional American dialects can vary widely, depending on the particular part of the region, the social and education background of the speakers, as well as the age group. What follows, however, are some basic characteristics that apply in general.

Southern

Southerners frequently confuse the second and third front vowels ɪ and e and substitute for ɪ as "pin" e as in "pen" and vice versa.

pin—pen	tin—ten	kin—Ken
bin—Ben	lid—lead	will—well
din—den	rid—red	till—tell
pick—peck	did—dead	sill—sell
big—beg	him—hem	rid—red
fill—fell	hill—hell	kilt—Celt
spill—spell	Sid—said	pig—peg

Sentences for Practice

1. Tell Will to hem it for him.
2. Pick ten big eggs.
3. Where has Ben been?
4. Evelyn sent him twenty-seven cents.
5. I don't get it.
6. Push the pin into the peg.
7. Ken filled his kin's big pig pen.
8. Will dug a well on the hill.
9. The din in Sid's den is dreadful.
10. Ben read the will.

Voice for Performance

Southerners should watch a tendency to nasalize vowels before nasal consonants. The section on Nasality and Denasality later in this chapter is a good one to work on.

iː	preen	beam	keen	dean	mean	seen
ɪ	pin	been	king	din	Ming	sing
e	pen	Ben	Ken	den	many	send
æ	pang	bang	can	dangle	mangle	sang
ɜː	earn	burn	fern	Myrna	learn	turn
ʌ	un	bungle	fun	monk	lunk	junk

uː	boom	moon	dune		room	June	soon
ɑː	bomb	mom	dominate		Ronald	John	calm

There is also a tendency to substitute long vowels for diphthongs. Go over the practice selections for diphthongs and make sure the second element is emphasized.

	eĭ	**aĭ**	**ɔĭ**	**oŭ**	**ɑŭ**
Example:	make	my	boy	go	out

New York

Make sure that the dental consonants **t**, **d**, **n**, **l** are made with the *tip* of the tongue rather than the *blade* of the tongue (the part right in back of the tip) and that the tip of the tongue is articulating against the gum ridge and not the back of the upper front teeth. Watch that the tip of the tongue does not pull back for the consonant **l**.

Make sure diphthongs are accurate: may **eĭ** (may) not **aĭ** (my).

Go over the specific rules for **ŋ** endings on pages 75–76.

Don't add a **g** sound after the nasal consonat **ŋ**. It's "ringing," not "ring ging."

Work on the exercises for the soft palate in the section on Nasality and Denasality.

Middle West

Watch the vowel **æ** when it is followed by a nasal consonant. The sound tends to flatten and nasalize.

Soften the **r** before another consonant and work on the exercises for the consonant **r**.

Work on the exercises for the soft palate in the section on Nasality and Denasality.

California

The speech of California used to be considered almost unaccented American English, but no longer. The so-called "Valley Girl" speech has not only taken hold in the San Fernando Valley in southern California where it originated, but has now spread across suburban America as well. It is generational, in that it is now mainly reflects the speech patterns of the twentysomethings and is seen as a clear linguistic dividing line between those in their forties and younger people. It is characterized by denasal tones and upward vocal inflexions in which final phrases end in a "question-like" intonation or slide downwards into vocal fry. Some linguists also call it "mall speech." Vocal fry is a term used to describe the sound that occurs when the voice is allowed to drop down on to the vocal cords instead of being placed forward in the frontal bones of the face. It is described as sounding like fat frying in a pan.

The difficulty here is vocal as well as speech-related, with some of the characteristics being voices pitched above or below optimal pitch, with vocal fry at the ends of final syllables and phrases. While this particular regional dialect has its counterpart in England with "Estuary English," young actors need to actively embrace an enormous amount of both ear training and vocal training to become adept at switching out of it for mainstream plays.

Work on optimal pitch, resonance, and tone placement is a must.

Specific Speech Problems

Whistling Sibilant s

Of all the common speech problems, a whistling sibilant **s** is probably the most irritating. It is also difficult to give a series of exercises that will be effective for everyone, because of the different physical makeup of each individual. The alignment of the jaw and teeth and the physical shape of the teeth can cause an **s** to whistle. In general, however, the following exercises have proved effective in most cases with regular and precise practice.

The **s-z** sounds are made with the tip of the tongue free and pointing towards the *front* of the upper gum ridge. Some individuals make this sound with the tip of the tongue behind the lower front teeth, but this can present a problem when the **s-z** consonants follow another tip of the tongue consonant such as **t-d-n-l**. For most people, it is best if the consonant **s-z** is made with the tip of the tongue pointing up rather than down. The sides of the tongue are touching the sides of the upper molars and the teeth are in line—one right on top of the other, the front teeth directly in line with the bottom teeth. *The teeth do not touch* although they may look as if they do, but they are directly in line, one of top of the other.

At first this position may seem awkward, and you may feel as if the jaw is jutting forward. Remember, however, that this position is for **s-z** *only* and is a very natural movement. Eating a pizza also requires the teeth to be in line when we bite into the crust as the jaw juts forward to bring the teeth into line. With practice this becomes second nature, and in most cases this adjustment alone will lessen or eliminate the whistle.

Exercises for Practice

You will need a mirror for this exercise so you can study your bite and how your teeth go together.

Bring the lower teeth in line with the upper teeth—you can test gently with your finger tip to see whether the line is exact. Don't let the teeth touch as this will cause tension in the jaw. Now bring the tip of the tongue up to the upper gum ridge and say **ts-ts-ts-ts-ts-ts-ts-ts-ts**. There should be a connection between the diaphragmatic breath and the release of the breath on the tip of the tongue, almost as if the little pant in the diaphragm is connected to the tip of the tongue. Repeat until this exercise is easy. The use of the consonant **t** helps to strengthen the tip of the tongue for the **s** sound and puts the tip of the tongue in the correct position.

Now practice the following one syllable words, holding the **t** for a moment and then releasing the breath on the tip of the tongue:

Initial

t-see	t-set	t-sand	t-soon	t-such	t-Sam	t-say
t-seat	t-sound	t-psalm	t-sow	t-sent	t-sigh	t-soul
t-son	t-sought	t-sue	t-sat	t-sow	t-seer	t-seep

t-static story	t-stirring steeple	t-still stare
t-stout stick	t-stooping stood	t-sturdy stock
t-stumbling step	t-steel stack	t-static style
t-sniveling sneak	t-sleeping slave	t-streaming strand
t-snarling snout	t-slurring slander	t-strict stress
t-snapping snip	t-slim sleeve	t-stray straw
t-sneaking snail	t-slippery slide	t-strong string

Medial

fencing master	lasting bluster	thirsty beasts
mustard plaster	pestering sister	fasting priests
castor frosting	grasping master	forsaken apostles
dancing lesson	passing fancies	bristling masts

Final

clasps	wreaths	juts	cakes	dents	sleeps
breaths	sheaths	wits	coats	leaf's	beats
healths	haunts	frosts	slats	crusts	kicks
laughs	foots	kites	plots	thirsts	trusts

Connections

seem strange	thief's score	save some	live seed
tube socks	some swan	sharp spear	last stop
lost song	same smile	best scene	just so
strict scruples	bed story	sun spot	big sister

Tongue Twister

Through rifts in the lofts,
The soft snow sifts.
Then the white sheet lifts
And the wind packs drifts.

Lisping

Lisping is sometimes caused by malocclusion of the teeth. In other words the upper and lower teeth don't line up properly so that the tongue either slides into
the space between the sides of the upper and lower teeth or juts on the front
teeth themselves instead of the gum ridge. If you have difficulties with your bite
you should consult an orthodontist. If you are undergoing orthodontia you will
probably want to wait until it is finished before embarking on correction. Even if
the condition of your bite is such that it causes problems, but can't be corrected
by orthodontia, it is possible that with determined practice you can overcome the
effects of a lisp and acquire fairly good sibilant sounds. It just takes practice.

Sometimes lisping is caused by a tongue-tie. If you look under your tongue, your will find the frenum, a muscular tissue that joins the tongue to the middle line of the floor of the mouth. If it is too short, it may be stretched by tongue exercises like the ones in Chapter II. If, howver, it is very short and prevents the tip of the tongue from freely moving up to the gum ridge for the consonants **t-d-n-l-tʃ-dʒ-r**, then a competent oral surgeon should be consulted. It is a very simple surgical procedure to have the frenum cut and it can be done in an office visit.

Exercises for Practice

Practice consonant combinations of **θ ð** and **s**. The tip of the tongue should be on the edge of the upper front teeth and free and pointing to the front of the upper gum ridge for the following word combinations:

thee—see	third—sir	than—sand
thin—sin	thump—sump	there—Sarah
then—sent	through—sue	Thor—soar
they—say	though—so	thick—stick
thank—sank	thaw—saw	thrall—Saul
thy—sigh	thought—sought	thine—sign

Sentences for Practice

1. Theda said that Susan thought mythical anthologies thoroughly silly.
2. The northwestern states still thirst for a southwest breath of rain.
3. In theory thiamine thoroughly soothes the slothful thyroid.
4. Thirty-six thousand Syrian soldiers thronged southwest through the Thracian suburbs.
5. Thankfully Arthur's health strengthened through the sixth of this month.

Tongue Twister

Six thick thistle sticks, six, thick thistle sticks.

The Leith police dismisseth us, the Leith police dismisseth us.

Red leather, yellow leather, red leather, yellow leather.

Poetry is the synthesis of hyacinths and biscuits.

Nasality and Denasality

These two voice problems tend to get lumped together under the heading of "nasality" when in fact they are opposites. Nasality is a condition in which the voice is produced through the nose with an unpleasant "twang" for all sounds. Denasality is caused by a *lack* of nasal resonance with all of the sounds coming from the mouth with the nasal resonators almost cut off as if the speaker were suffering from a bad head cold. The common denominator for both conditions is the *soft palate*.

In English there are three nasal consonants, **m n ŋ**, which are emitted through the nose with the soft palate *lowered*. These consonants give resonance and color to the vowels and diphthongs by association and should be full and resonant. All other sounds in English are produced with the soft palate *lifted*. Obviously, the soft palate needs to be very flexible to handle the demands of lifting and lowering within the same word as in "man, ring, none." To correct a problem with *both* nasality and denasality involves strengthening the soft-palate.

First of all, using a mirror, look into your mouth to the back of the throat behind the tongue. You should see the arch of the roof of the mouth and the *uvula*, which is the little tag of flesh than hangs down at the back of the throat. This is the end of the soft palate. Notice whether it is very long and heavy and seems to touch the back of the tongue. That may be a sign that the soft palate is not lifting for the non-nasal sounds.

Exercises for the Soft Palate

1. Open your mouth and drop the jaw for the position of **ɑː** (ah). Begin to pant from your diaphragmatic muscles just under the sternum or breast bone. Start slowly and then increase speed. Watch in your mirror the movement of the uvula, which flips up and down with the intake and the release of air as you pant.

2. Drop the jaw and begin to inhale and exhale on a **kɑː**. Feel the soft palate lift and lower on **kɑː** with the inhalation and exhalation.

3. Yawn, keeping the tip of the tongue behind the lower front teeth. The uvula will tip up behind the *oro-pharynx* (the back of the throat) and the space around the end of the soft palate should arch and lift. This lifting of the soft palate on the yawn stretches the muscles and helps tone them for the task of closing for the nasal consonants and opening for the other vowel and consonant sounds.

4. The soft palate is affected by the shaping of the vowels with the lips and the tongue. For the Front vowels the soft palate lowers slightly, for the Middle vowels it is relaxed and neutral, ad for the Back vowels the soft palate lifts slightly. Remember for *all* vowel sounds the tip of the tongue should remain behind the lower front teeth, which helps keep the soft palate up for all vowel sounds to prevent a nasal "twang."

Round the lips for **uː** and then slightly spread them in a smile for **iː**

uː - iː - uː - iː - uː - iː - uː - iː

ɔː - iː - ɔː - iː - ɔː - iː - ɔː - iː

ɑː - iː - ɑː - iː - ɑː - iː - ɑː - iː

Intone: me, may, my, mow, moo feeling the sensation of vibration on your lips and through the nose

Intone: **ŋɑː - ŋɑː - ŋɑː - ŋɑː**, feeling the sensation of vibration on the soft palate and through the nose.

Nasality

Nasality is caused by the voice being directed through the nose for all sounds, which creates a twanging, honking quality in the voice. It is usually caused by a lack of flexibility in the soft palate which prevents the soft palate from lifting to cut off the sound from the nasal cavity. In English the soft palate should only lower for the nasal consonants **m n ŋ**. The following exercises are to develop coordination in the soft palate for both the nasal consonants and the other sounds of English.

Exercises for Practice

1. Intone on the consonant **m**. Feel the sound coming through the nose with your fingers. Now slide into the vowel **ɑː**. There should be no vibration in the nose for the **ɑː**. Alternate between these two sounds: **m - ɑː - m - ɑː - m - ɑː**.

2. Yawn downward, making sure that the tip of the tongue does not pull back but stays behind the lower front teeth. Check in the mirror to observe the uvula lift up at the peak of the yawn. This stretches the muscles in the soft palate and helps it develop flexibility.

3. In the following exercises make sure the soft palate lifts *up* for all the vowels and drops *down* for the three nasal consonants **m n ŋ**.

Let the lips come together for **m** then drop the jaw for **ɑː**. Let the jaw remain in place for **ɑː** as you bring up the *tip* of the tongue for **n**. Now drop the tip of the tongue down for **ɑː** and let the back of the tongue arch up to the soft palate for **ɑː** and again let the jaw drop down for the vowel **ɑː**

m	ɑː	m	ɑː	m	ɑː
ɑː	m	ɑː	m	ɑː	m
n	ɑː	n	ɑː	n	ɑː
ɑː	n	ɑː	n	ɑː	n
ŋ	ɑː	ŋ	ɑː	ŋ	ɑː
ɑː	ŋ	ɑː	ŋ	ɑː	ŋ

5. Intone on the **ŋ** sound of the words "hung," allowing the voice to ride up into the upper register. Feel the sensation of a yawn in the soft palate, drop the back of the tongue down into the position for the vowel **ɑː**.

ŋɑː	ŋɑː	ŋɑː	ŋɑː
ŋoŭ	ŋoŭ	ŋoŭ	ŋoŭ
ŋuː	ŋuː	ŋuː	ŋu
ŋɔː	ŋɔː	ŋɔː	ŋɔː
ŋiː	ŋiː	ŋː	ŋiː

Denasality

The denasal voice sounds very much as if the person had a bad head cold. It is caused by a lack of nasal resonance. This can be the result of a variety of conditions, such as a chronic case of sinusitis, a series of colds that linger, a broken nose, a deviated septum (this means that one side of the nose is blocked and interferes with the breathing), or adenoids, which are an enlarged mass of tissue in the nasopharynx. Adenoids can cause breathing problems because they obstruct one's ability to breathe through the nose and force one to breath through the mouth. If uncorrected, enlarged adenoids can cause hearing problems and even physical changes in the dental-facial structure.

If you suffer from chronic denasality, consult a reputable ear, eye, nose, and throat specialist to find out the cause. Only when any chronic condition is cleared up can voice exercises have any real effect.

Exercises for Denasality

1. Open your mouth and yawn: feel how the soft palate lifts up. Now say **ɑː** feeling the same lift in the soft palate. Now close the lips and say **m**, feeling the vibrations on the lips with the sound coming through the nose. Try to sense the soft palate lowering on **m**. Keep alternating between **m**—feeling the soft palate lift for **ɑː** and lower for **m**.

    Now repeat the exercise substituting the consonants **n** and **ŋ**. Now repeat the exercise but do not say the sounds—just repeat the muscular activity feeling the soft palate lift and lower.

2. All of the exercises for nasality should be practiced for denasality as well because they involve coordination of the soft palate. Try to feel the vibrations on the nose with your fingers to determine if there is nasal resonance on the nasal consonants.

The Tense Jaw

Tension or rigidity in the jaw is a common complaint but the description of the problem is often misleading. The jaw itself is a loose bony mandible that fits into the sides of the upper skull. As it is the part of the body most often found missing when skeletons are found, it stands to reason that the jaw itself isn't tight. The tension is in the intrinsic muscles that move the jaw up and down and forward that are tense and tight.

    The jaw fits into small grooves located at the sides of the skull just below the opening of the ear. If you place your fingers at the side of your head and then drop your jaw and move it up and down, you will be able to feel where the jaw inserts into the skill. If you have access to a real skull, take a look at the grooves at the sides of the skull where the jaw slips in. Notice how easily it dislodges and how easily it drops down unless you hold it up. If, as you can see, the jaw is actually loosely attached to the skull, how is it that when people speak, it moves so little?

Problems With the Jaw

The seriousness of tension and related problems with the jaw is now recognized as a health problem that afflicts many people beyond the province of voice work. It can be responsible for severe headaches, ulcers, backache, and other related

disorders and many people go from doctor to doctor, submitting themselves to
all sorts of drugs and sometimes surgery for ailments brought on by problems
with the jaw. There is now a medical category that some of these disorders fit
into: called *Tempular Mandibular Joint Syndrome* or TMJ.

TMJ

TMJ can be caused by a number of things, ranging from improper bite due to
malformation of the teeth, thumb sucking (yes, believe it or not some adults
still suck their thumbs), grinding the teeth when asleep, poor posture, and even
holding the head in a strained position such as when talking on the phone with
the receiver tucked between the shoulder and the chin. It can also be the result
of an accident which caused a blow to the jaw, knocking it off its hinge. Whatever
the cause, if you suffer from a grinding sensation in the jaw area when you open
and close your mouth, pain the in jaw area, or a clicking or sticking of the jaw
when you open it, you should consult a dentist who specializes in diagnosis and
treatment of TMJ. Often they will construct a special bite plate that can help
bring the jaw into better alignment.

Exercises for practice

If there is no medical reason for a tight, tense jaw, the condition can be improved
by articulatory exercise. The goal is to achieve more flexibility in articulation
through shaping the vowels and consonants with the lips and the tongue. This is
done by allowing the tip of the tongue to move freely up to the gum ridge in order to pronounce the tip of the tongue consonants **t-d**, **n**, **l**, **s-z**, **ʃ-ʒ**. The tongue
then drops behind the lower front teeth for the vowels and finally the back of the
tongue will arch up on the **k g ŋ** consonants and flatten for the vowels sounds.

Check to see whether you hold your teeth together when you are not speaking. The teeth should *never* touch whether you are speaking or silent. Remember:
LIPS TOGETHER TEETH APART is a little mantra that all TMJ sufferers should
repeat daily.

Chapter VII
Keeping Your Voice Healthy

For my voice,
I have lost it with hollering and singing of anthems

Henry IV, Part 2 *William Shakespeare*

We don't give much thought to our voice until something goes wrong with it or until we are made aware that there is something wrong with it. This may come about during the rehearsal period, just before an opening night, or even during the run of the show. Whenever it occurs, it becomes the main focus of our attention as well as that the director and the management.

The purpose of this chapter is to focus on vocal hygiene. We will discuss what to do in case of vocal trouble, when to get medical attention, with whom to consult, and some helpful hints for keeping the voice in shape.

First, the vocal mechanism is made up of living tissue and is subject to and reflective of the same stresses as the rest of the body. A cold, fatigue, stress, air pollution, allergies, hormonal changes, weight loss or gain, certain medication, or change in the amount and kinds of vocal usage can have an adverse effect on the voice. Certain diseases can also be reflected in the voice. Chronic hoarseness, persistent cough, change in vocal quality, voice loss, and tightness or pain when speaking should all be reported to a physician.

Usually an actor first becomes aware of vocal difficulty when he or she can least afford to, either late in rehearsal or in performance. When the voice is needed the most is often when vocal problems manifest themselves. This is because the voice is being used for longer periods under the pressure of performance. In addition, the conditions found in most rehearsal spaces, which are frequently dry, dusty, cold or overheated, exacerbate the problem. On tour, the effects of travel in dehydrating jet aircraft can add further complications. An actor may also experience vocal difficulties when beginning acting training or when portraying characters that require a higher or lower pitch or as a result of a great deal of shouting and screaming in emotional scenes. Whatever the cause, the results are very trying for the actor.

The first priority for any voice user is to prevent vocal problems by keeping the voice healthy. This means keeping the body healthy through proper diet, exercise, rest, and refraining from smoking or abusing alcohol and controlled substances. It also means maintaining a sound vocal technique and avoiding vocal abuse, whether in speaking or singing. The following are examples of vocal abuse in both the speaking and the singing voice.

Yelling and Screaming

Whether you are cheering your favorite team, calling the dog, disciplining children, trading stock, or playing King Lear in the storm scene, screaming without proper vocal support can be very dangerous for the voice. Because a scream or shout is an emotional response, it is hard to approach it with cool detachment. Basically one should remember that the first impulse must be to breathe in, support the breath with your abdominal muscles, and let the breath fuel the emotion that produces the scream or shout. Don't exhale on the line, but keep the breath behind the tone. Try to place the voice in the frontal bones of the face, far forward and off the vocal cords. Focus on the voiced consonants, feeling the vibration where the sounds are made. Don't tighten the jaw and above all don't tense the neck muscles to support the sound.

Making a Hard Glottal Attack

This is can be caused by tensing the throat muscles instead of taking a breath before speaking or by stopping the voice in the middle of a phrase, then speaking again without taking a breath. It can also be caused by laughing in an abusive manner. Breathe before speaking, support and keep the placement of the voice forward.

Speaking in a Noisy Environment

This is a common cause of vocal abuse. Speaking in an airplane, a noisy car, a crowded room, or against a background of ambient noise such as crowd scenes can cause the speaker to push and strain the voice to be heard. A simple technique is to just lift the pitch up over the existing sound level rather than increasing the volume.

Coughing and Excessive Throat Clearing

This can be a vicious circle. Vocal abuse can cause excess mucous to form which leads to throat clearing and coughing, which in turn causes more vocal abuse. If you feel your voice in the throat or if it feels scratchy, blow through your lips, making them vibrate on a comfortable higher pitch ending on a **m-m-m**. Now say "uh-hum-m," feeling the voice vibrating on the lips. Keep humming on that easy comfortable pitch, keeping the voice forward in the "mask" or the frontal bones of the face. There should be no sense of strain in the throat. When you speak, keep the voice forward aiming for the back of the upper front teeth.

Grunting While Exercising and Lifting

Lifting heavy objects causes the vocal cords to adduct or come together. Grunting can damage the voice by adding further strain on the vocal cords. Use care in lifting heavy objects while speaking. If you are directed to lift a heavy object, such as the body of another actor, make sure you are able to put it down before attempting a long difficult speech or singing.

Calling Others—Friends, Children, Pets—from a Distance

When you call from a distance, even hailing a taxi, be sure to take a breath first and then lift the pitch slightly, keeping the voice forward in the mask. Feel the breath behind the voice, letting the voice ride on the breath.

Using a Pitch Level That is Too Low

Speaking on a pitch that is too low is one of the most common forms of vocal abuse. This is true of both men and women. The reasons are usually cultural. A low sultry voice is thought to be sexy in a woman; a deep voice is thought to be very macho in a man.

Most people agree that a high pitched voice is offensive to the ear, but serious vocal problems can develop when the pitch is artificially maintained at a pitch that is inappropriate for the speaker's own vocal range. Placing the voice on optimal pitch (see Chapter IV: Resonance) will result in a voice that is comfortable and healthy for the speaker as well as pleasant to the listening ear. Remember that our own perception of pitch may be inaccurate as we don't really hear ourselves as we really sound. When speaking on your optimal pitch, your voice may actually sound lower to an audience than it sounds to the speaker.

Vocal Fry

Vocal fry is the name given to a quality of sound which is produced at a low pitch and in which the voice seems to rest on the vocal cords. This occurs more commonly with female speakers. Unfortunately vocal fry is becoming part of the linguistic pattern of many younger American speakers.

The problem for the performer is that the voice is produced below the optimal pitch, which makes it harder to hear and causes ends of sentences to trail off and become unintelligible. Vocal fry can also lead to vocal abuse and damage to the vocal cords when an actor tries to project the voice at that low placement and pitch.

To combat vocal fry, work on the exercises in *Chapter IV: Resonance*. Try taking a few lines of poetry, there are lots of samples in this book, and read them as though you were chanting. Be sure to breathe before you start to speak and at the end of each line of verse. Notice where you place your voice when you chant, and then see if you can speak the verse at the same pitch and with the same placement in the frontal bones of your face that you feel when chanting. Also let one word run into another word without separating them. Connected speech should be one smooth stream connected by a breath at pauses.

Speaking in an Abusive Manner During a Cold, Upper Respiratory Infection, or Allergy Attack

If you begin to lose your voice or if your throat feels scratchy during these infections, it is a signal from your body to rest the voice. If you have an important performance, consult an otolaryngologist before making any final decision to perform.

Smoking Excessively—Including Marijuana

The dangers of smoking to one's health are so well-known that it should hardly need repeating here. Some performers believe that smoking marijuana is less harmful than tobacco. It is not. The effect on the lungs and the vocal tract are even worse than cigarettes. Furthermore they interfere with the intricate muscular interactions of the vocal apparatus.

For nonsmokers who must perform in a smoky environment, try to insist that smokers refrain from lighting up while you are singing or speaking. If your character smokes on stage, try to use very low tar and nicotine cigarettes and practice until you can fake the inhale, holding the smoke in the mouth and then exhaling. It is also possible to use cigarettes as props, fiddling with them, picking them up, putting them down, etc. Be imaginative and try to use a cigarette as a prop only when absolutely necessary for your character because it is called for in the script. Some actors use herbal cigarettes as substitutes, but I have no data on whether or not they are harmful.

Speaking With Inadequate Breath Support

This is usually combined with tension and poor posture. Try to remember that the impulse to speak should first trigger the impulse to breathe. Breathe before you speak and don't let all your breath out on the first word or syllable. When you come to the end of a phrase, breathe on top of the breath you have taken. Remember that air is FREE! You don't have to use up all the air in your lungs before you are entitled to another breath. You should always feel as if you had some air left in your lungs when you come to the end of a phrase and not have to gasp for another breath. Keep your body in alignment and let the breath come from just below the ribs, feeling the ribs expand with the initial breath.

Performing Without a Sufficient Warm-Up

Allow yourself enough time before a performance or rehearsal to warm up the voice. You should know the most effective warm-up exercise for your own voice and allow sufficient time to do them.

Talking Excessively After a Performance

Actors and singers frequently devote a large amount of time talking with friends after the show—frequently in a loud and smoky environment. If you have a vocally demanding role, be careful how much time you spend talking while socializing after a performance.

Gastroesophageal Reflux Disease

Gastroesophageal Reflux Disease (GERD) is a chronic condition that is caused by the inability of a ring-like structure at the lower part of the esophagus to tighten, allowing stomach acid to splash up into the esophagus. It may be perceived as a burning sensation deep in the throat, hoarseness, difficulty swallowing, the feeling of a lump in the throat that does not seem to go away, a frequent perceived need to cough or clear the throat, or a persistent acid taste in the throat or mouth. There can be a change in pitch, particularly at the upper end of the range. It is frequently worse in the morning and improves as the day progresses. While it is not usually life threatening, it can aggravate asthma or other respiratory problems and can be a real misery for voice professionals.

GERD can be diagnosed by an x-ray of the upper digestive tract, or the physician may use an instrument called an endoscope to look into the esophagus and vocal tract. You doctor may also order a 24-hour acid test to measure the amount of acid in the stomach, as well as a range of other tests.

The principal treatment is a change in lifestyle and the use of antacids. Changing the diet to reduce acid-producing food and not eating two to three hours before bed are critical to healing. Although there is medication available, the greatest relief occurs through changes in diet and behavior. Also, according to some doctors, allergies may also be responsible for some cases of GERD.

The following are some of the changes in diet and lifestyle that can help to control GERD:
• Avoid cigarettes, caffeine and alcohol
• Avoid fried, spicy and fatty foods as well as chocolate, peppermint, spearmint, citrus, and tomato-based foods

- Eat small meals high in protein and carbohydrates and don't eat less than three hours before bedtime
- Lose weight, if needed and avoid tight clothing
- Raise the head of your bed by about 6 to 8 inches
- Take antacids as directed by your doctor

Chapter VIII
The Electronic Voice

Halloo your name to the reverberate hills
And make the babbling gossip of the air
Cry out 'Olivia!'"

Twelfth Night *William Shakespeare*

Although the focus of this book is on training the actor's voice for the live the-ater, a working professional actor frequently encounters the use of microphones in his or her work in radio, television, and film. While there is not a great deal of mystery in the use of microphones for film and television, today's actor fre-quently encounters a growing dependence on microphones in the live theater as well. While the specifics of microphone technology is the province of specialists in the field of sound design, actors should be aware that the primary function of sound design is to amplify and augment the sound of the actor's voice in the theater and be able to accommodate themselves to it.

While still controversial in some circles, the use of microphones in the live the-ater, is widespread and growing. The reasons given by producers and directors are:

1. Today's audiences are used to television and have difficulty listening to the live actor's voice without wanting to turn up the volume.
2. Many actors have been working in television and film for most of their careers and are unable to project their voices in a large theater.
3. The size of many new theaters inhibit the actor's ability to project.
4. Many new theaters don't have the acoustics of older theaters. (A British the-ater director told me rather sadly, that with the advent of the new acoustical science, theater acoustics are worse now than a century or two ago. He noted that the Olivier Theatre, which was built within the last thirty years and is the largest theater in London's new Royal National Theatre complex, mikes many

of its productions because it is difficult to hear the actors in many sections of the house due to dead spots.)

Whether the choice of miking in the theater is the fault of the actors, the producers, theater architects, or the public, it seems that miking a show is here to stay. The question is, just how does that affect the voice and speech work of the actors? Should performers just forget about projection and diction and let the mike do it all the work for them? Has the use of electronic amplification made theater voice training redundant?

For an answer to these questions, I interviewed four of Broadway's leading sound engineers, Abe Jacobs, Otts Munderloh, Tom Morse, and Brian Marsh to get their opinions on the subject. Their replies were candid, heartfelt, and to the point. Briefly, here is a synthesis of what they all had to say. You may find their observations surprising.

The Purpose of Miking

The purpose of miking is to reach where voice and acoustics are a problem and not to blast the audience with sound. It is to augment rather than replace the actor's voice. The function of a good amplification system is to enable the audience to hear and understand what is being said on the stage; the goal is to make the sound in the listening area as easy for the audience to hear in the back row as in the front row.

Problems with Miking

One of the chief problems with miking is that producers, directors, and actors believe that the microphone is supposed to solve all the problems of the theater space. Theater owners and producers put on shows designed for small theaters in theaters designed for 3,000 or more people and expect miking to do the trick.

Sound systems are frequently blamed for the audience's inability to hear when the real problem is the actor's lack of vocal training, especially if they are film or television actors with no experience on the stage. No amount of miking can compensate for poor articulation and using an optimal pitch that is so low that it limits the dynamic range of the voice.

There are also complaints about actors who feel that their job is to be real, rather than to be heard, leaving that responsibility to the sound engineer.

In musicals, it is often difficult to hear the words of the lyrics because the orchestration of instruments is frequently at the same pitch or quality as the voices. The instruments should have the same vocal tone, or vocal range as the singer's voices.

Another reason why there is an increased reliance on microphones in musicals is because orchestrations have been replacing acoustic pianos, which were usually at the center of the orchestra, with the one or more electronic keyboards.

Helpful Microphone Hints for Actors

• Speak on stage as if you are wearing earphones or an iPod and had to talk over the sound to be heard.
• Actors frequently believe they are already screaming and shouting and can't believe that they still can't be heard at the back of the house. Screaming and shouting do not insure that the audience can understand you. Resonance and articulation carry in the theater, not just volume.
• Emphasis should be on clarity and this is the responsibility of the actor
• In a musical one should be able to understand the words
• Actors should pay special attention to consonants, especially plosives at the ends of words or phrases
• Actors with vocal training help other actors with little training by establishing the intensity and energy required by the speaking voice on stage

All four of the sound designers I spoke with had horror stories of actors who could not or would not project or articulate onstage while demanding their deficiencies be overcome electronically. They also were full of admiration for performers whose vocal artistry and technique enhanced the productions in which they appeared and made their jobs deeply satisfying. Mickey Rooney, George Rose, Chita Rivera, Colm Wilkinson were some of the favorites named; the other unfortunates shall be nameless.

To sum up, the sound engineer can only enhance, amplify, and project voices that are already articulate and supported. They can not make up for a deficiency in vocal technique. If the actor can project as far as the fifth or sixth row with clarity, then the sound engineer can begin to augment the sound; if he can't, there will be trouble. A sound engineer cannot put in a consonant or a dropped end of a phrase; he can only amplify what is there.

Chapter IX
Special Voice Demands on the Actor

Pray God, your voice, like a piece of uncurrent gold,
be not cracked within the ring.

Hamlet *William Shakespeare*

There are some vocal demands that are particular to stage actors. This chapter doesn't address all of these demands, but here some that can cause problems.

The Shout and the Scream

This is a very difficult subject to cover adequately in a book because one really should have a teacher present, if only to prevent overdoing and abuse. Always remember that in anything that involves the voice, if it hurts *don't do it*! A scream or a shout is an emotional response that is hard to approach it with cool detachment. Keep focused and remember support the voice with the breath.

The Shout
Breathe in and hold on to the breath. Your breath is your power and must fuel the emotion behind the scream or shout. Don't inhale, exhale, and then shout. You want the breath behind the sound. Feel the abdominal muscles tense with the breath and then sharply release the breath on the sound.

Exercise for Practice
Take a breath, support, and then say: **hɑ:** with a sharp abdominal release. Then repeat **hɑ: hɑ:** again with a sharp abdominal release. Then **hɑ: hɑ: hɑ: hɑ:** with each release on **hɑ:** like a pant.

Place the voice in the frontal bones of the face, far forward and off the vocal cords. Try to focus on the voiced consonants, feeling the vibration on the sounds. There should be no sensation of the voice in the throat.

Practice

> **mɑː mɑː mɑː bɑː bɑː bɑː nɑː nɑː nɑː**
> **hɑː hɑː hɑː vɑː vɑː vɑː dɑː dɑː dɑː**

Practice (breath)

Practice Phrases (Breathe before each word)

> Hey!
> Hey! You!!
> Taxi!
> Help!
> No! Get out!
> Sit down!!

Selections for Practice

Hickey: I've got to tell you! You being the way you are now gets my goat. It's all wrong!

> *The Iceman Cometh* Eugene O'Neill

Stanley: Stel-lahh! STELL -AHHHH!

> *A Streetcar Named Desire* Tennessee Williams

Vanya: Let me go Elena! Let me go!

> *Uncle Vanya* Anton Chehkov

A horse! A horse! My kingdom for a horse!

> *Richard III* William Shakespeare

Hence, home you idle creatures, get you home!

> *Julius Caesar* William Shakespeare

For England, Harry, and St. George!

> *Henry V* William Shakespeare

Awake, Malcolm and Donaldbain, Awake!

> *Macbeth* William Shakespeare

The Scream

For a scream, remember to place the voice high in the face, above the soft palate. Don't push from the throat—support from the ribcage. There should be no pain but don't overdo it. Don't let directors push you to repeat a high-pitched scream over and over again. Learn to mark it, which is a term that singers use to describe singing down an octave or not projecting fully to save their voices during rehearsal. Be sure to open your mouth and spread your lips to let the sound out. Keep the supported breath *behind* the scream; don't release all your breath but keep the sound supported.

Practice on a bare stage or in an empty room, until you feel you can do the scream without tensing your throat. Don't overdo it!

Practice

Help!!! Help!!!
Stop! Thief!!!
"Murder!" "Murder!"
Run!!!

The Stage Whisper

A whisper on stage is not a real whisper, which is articulation on the breath. It is in fact, a resonated tone with lots of breath over the tone.

Practice: Keep the voice forward in the mask and release extra breath as you speak. Check with your director or fellow actors sitting in the theater during rehearsal to make sure that you are both keeping the voice forward so it can be heard, and releasing enough breath to give the illusion of a whisper.

Practice:

(Make sure you breathe after each phrase)

Shhh!   Is that you?   I can't see you in the dark?

Be quiet!   I think I hear someone coming.

Quick! In here!! Get down!

Hush! They're in the next room!

Character Voices

Rough Voice

If the character you play is meant to have a rough, gravely voice, be careful that you don't actually push your own voice down on the larynx to get the same effect. You must produce the illusion of a rough gravely voice and not affect the real thing. Practice placing your voice forward and hum on **m** while tensing the soft palate. Repeat these placement exercises until you can get the sound you want without hurting your voice. Remember to support the sound with breath. Rule number one is if it hurts—*don't do it.*

Practice

Murderer: My lord, his throat is cut; that I did for him.
> *Macbeth* William Shakespeare

Nasal Voice

This one is fairly easy and doesn't do any vocal damage.

Just place the voice is the naso-pharynx. Keep the soft palate fairly high and tense and speak with the voice coming through your nose.

Practice

But in a sieve I'll thither sail,
And, like a rat without a tail,
I'll do, I'll do, and I'll do.
> *Macbeth* William Shakespeare

High Pitched Voice

You can give the effect of a high voice without actually having to go very high, but keeping the voice in the head resonator and minimizing the chest resonator.

Practice

Ariel: All hail, great master, grave sir, hail!
> *The Tempest* William Shakespeare

Ghosts: Dream on thy cousins smother'd in the Tower.
Thy nephews' souls bid thee despair and die.
> *Richard III* William Shakespeare

Low Pitched Voice

A low voice can be obtained by bringing the voice very forward, but emphasizing the chest resonator. Be careful with this one that you don't push the voice down on the vocal cords. Practice keeping your ribs expanded as well, as this will give more overtones.

Practice

Caliban: This island's mine by Sycorax my mother,
Which thou tak'st from me.
> *The Tempest* William Shakespeare

Dialects

This is a complex subject. As there are so many plays that are performed with dialects from Great Britain, a British dictionary is a good investment and can be purchased online.

In general I advise actors to begin making their own personal library of dialects—recording from television programs or videos, and making recordings of willing subjects with interesting accents. There are a variety of dialect tapes and CDs on the market that are very useful, but some of them are recorded by the same non-native speaker doing more than one dialect. Be sure to supplement your dialect CDs with those of native speakers of that dialect. Be very specific. If you are doing a play like *Rat in the Skull* by Ron Hutchinson you don't want to do an southern Irish dialect from the Republic of Ireland for the RUC police officer from Northern Ireland.

Pronunciation

It is the actor's responsibility to find the correct pronunciation for the words in the text of a play. If you are in a British play, check British dictionaries for correct pronunciations. Birmingham is the name of a city in both America and the United Kingdom, but they are pronounced differently. I once sat through a production of a play in England that was set in Birmingham, Alabama, but the British actor's pronounced it without the "h" as they do in England. It was unintentionally hilarious to the Americans in the audience.

Don't rely on the director or your fellow actors—you are the one up there on the stage. If you are in doubt about the specific pronunciation of a place name, such as a town, a street, or a particular building in a play, spend the money and make a long distance call to the local public library of the town in which the play takes place. You will find the librarian will be thrilled to help you. For example, if you are in a play set in New York City and Houston Street is mentioned—you need to make sure you don't get caught pronouncing the street with the same pronunciation as the city in Texas. It's not **hjuːstn,** it's **haʊstn.** There will be New Yorkers in the audience—trust me—who will let you know if you get it wrong.

Acting in Period Costume

Breathing in a Corset

Actors often express concern that wearing a period costume, with the corseting required, will interfere with their ability to breathe. This should not be the case. Remember that actors and actresses on the stage have for centuries have worn corseting and performed (without amplification it should be noted) in houses that were often much larger than most contemporary houses. Wearing a corset should not present any problems if a few simple rules are followed.

Fit

Work with the costumer to make sure that your corset is fitted properly. If you feel the corset is too small, say so. It is best, of course, if the corset is made specifically for the individual actor. Sometimes in small theaters, actors go into the costume shop and rummage in a box labeled "corsets" and pull one out that looks like it might fit or is attractive. If you are given a used corset, go to the costumer and ask to have it properly fitted. They are trained to do this and are usually very helpful if there is a problem.

Lacing

Just before you are to be laced into the corset—BREATHE IN—allowing the lower ribs to expand—then let your dresser lace you up. This will give you adequate space for the breath.

Note: If there are still problems with breathing after this, the fault probably lies with the vocal technique (or lack of it) of the actor and not with the corset. Chest breathing rather than lower diaphragmatic breathing is usually the cause.

Chapter X
An Approach to Text

And the moral of that is, "Take care of the sense, and the sounds will take care of themselves."
Alice in Wonderland *Lewis Carroll*

When an actor encounters the words of the text in rehearsal, his job is to convey the meaning of the text as expressed by the character he is playing. He must dig into the sense the author is trying to convey, find the thought and feeling behind the words, and make choices based on his inner conviction of the truth being expressed. Often he finds that despite his best efforts, he is not communicating the ideas that he thinks he is and can get locked into a speech pattern that is difficult to break.

The following elements are *guides* to help the actor explore the text and to enable him or her to communicate the meaning of the text to an audience.

Stress

In the living life of a language, some words are emphasized more than others, depending on the meaning behind what is said. One of the ways in which we communicate the sense lying beneath the actual words we say is to place emphasis on the word or "stress," which is defined as "extra force used in speaking on a particular word or syllable." In the following sentence, notice how the meaning shifts with the stress:

Example:
Mary had a green dress.
Mary *had* a green dress.
Mary had *a* green dress.
Mary had a *green* dress.
Mary had a green *dress*.

In the simple sentence "John and Mary should have gone to Spain," Read the sentence and give emphasis to each word in turn. See how a shift of stress not only affects the meaning, but the pronunciation of the word.

> *John* and Mary should have gone to Spain.
> John *and* Mary should have gone to Spain
> John and *Mary* should have gone to Spain
> John and Mary *should* have gone to Spain
> John and Mary should *have* gone to Spain.
> John and Mary should have *gone* to Spain.
> John and Mary should have gone *to* Spain.
> John and Mary should have gone to *Spain*.

The meaning of the sentence is determined by the change in stress, but the choice of *which* words to stress depends on the sense the actor wants to convey. Any word may be stressed if it important to the sense being expressed in the text although there are some general guidelines.

Nouns are usually important words because they are the names of things we are thinking about.

> Example: *Philip* missed the last train.
> Philip missed the last *train*.

Verbs convey action.

> Example: Philip *missed* the last train.

Adjectives and *Adverbs* modify nouns and verbs and they may describe kind or manner in a way that is essential to the sense.

> Example: Philip missed the *last* train.

Articles are usually subordinated unless necessary to the sense; therefore when an article is stressed it is usually to denote something special about the noun that it modifies.

> Example: Philip missed *the* last train.

The decision of which word to stress in the sentence "Philip missed the last train." would be determined by what meaning you were trying to convey.

Although it is a sure sign of an inexperienced reader when the articles are stressed indiscriminately, there are instances where one does stress an article.

> Example: Bill: You caught some fish?
> John: I caught *a* fish.

Prepositions are usually unstressed except when the meaning being communicated makes them important. Lincoln's "Gettysburg Address" is a prime example.

> *"that government **of** the people, **by** the people and **for** the people shall not perish from the earth"*

Pronouns take the place of nouns and should only be stressed when contrast is indicated.

> Example: The new members of the cast are John, James, and Joan. *She* seems talented.

Connectives are generally unstressed but may require emphasis under some circumstances.

> Example: Before you leave this house you will wash the dishes, make the beds, sweep the floor, carry out the garbage, *and* (long pause) anything else I can think of.

Auxiliary Verbs and forms of the verb "to be" are usually not of much interest unless they serve words of higher interest.

> Example: You *will* go to work today.

A good rule to remember concerning stress was suggested by Lewis Carrol, the author of *Alice in Wonderland*:

> "My rule for knowing which word to lean on is the word that tells you something new, something that is different from what you expected."

Emphasize: The new idea or the contrasting idea.
Subdue: The old idea.

Antithesis. When two words are *contrasting*, both words get equal stress:

hot and cold	rain or shine	salt and pepper
black and white	back and forth	silver and gold
up and down	left and right	male and female

> They have their *exits* and their *entrances,*
> And *one* man in his time plays *many* parts.
>> *As You Like It* William Shakespeare

Intonation

Intonation is the rising and falling of the pitch of the voice when speaking. It is also a vocal quality that indicates the use of a word for a specific meaning. The intonation of a language is also its melody pattern or tune. Rising and falling glides on individual syllables in a group are among the outstanding characteristics of English intonation. These glides occur invariably on stressed syllables.

In most phrases, English intonation usually begins above the optimal pitch of the voice on the first stressed syllable and moves in a general direction down to the last stressed syllable on which the glide usually occurs.

> *Example:* Children are happy at school.
> *Are* children happy at school?

Intonation Patterns

1. A simple falling intonation indicates that the statement is either a statement, a command, or a decision.

> *Example:* Go to the store.
> I'm going home, I'm tired.

2. A rising intonation indicates an unfinished thought, uncertainty, and question asked without a question word, surprise.

> *Example:* Go to the store *and...* (the statement is unfinished as the person speaking thinks of things wanted to be picked up at the store).

- an uncertainty

> "I'm not sure...

- a question asked without a question word

> You're sure?

- or a statement of simple surprise.

> "It's you!"

3. Level intonation indicates suspended thought, awe, wonder, deep controlled emotion.

> *Example:* I wonder…It's beautiful.
> Please don't go.

4. Circumflex intonation is a rising and falling of the voice on the same syllables. It indicates sarcasm, scorn, irony, surprise, subtlety of mind and mood, incredulity.

> *Example:* Men and women are alike.
> Do you *really* think men and women are alike?
> *All* men and *all* women?
> What an *extraordinary* idea!

Again it should be emphasized that these are guides, not rules. However actors should remember that an audience can't automatically understand the meaning inherent in a text but must rely on the actor's voice to do it for him.

Inflection

When a thought is unfinished or there is a question the voice moves up:

> Did you know…?
> Oh, really?

Intonation, inflection and stress in plays are often indicated by underlining or italics and can involve stress as well as inflection.

> Do you *really* mean that?
> He's not *that* hard to please.
> It's not for *us* to say!
> *You're* the one he wants.

Intonation, inflection, and stress provide nuances of thought and intention, enabling the audience to understand the deeper meaning behind a line.

The following lines from plays contain the playwright's indication of intonation inflection and stress:

> Be happy—if you're not even *happy* what's so good about surviving?
> *Rosencrantz and Guildenstern Are Dead* Tom Stoppard

Emma: Ever think of me?
Jerry: I don't need to think of you.
Emma: Oh?
Jerry: I don't need to *think* of you.
          Betrayal Harold Pinter

Stanley: Hey, canary bird! Toots! Get OUT of the BATHROOM!
          A Streetcar Named Desire Tennessee Williams

You got to take your chance for happiness.
You got to grab it.
You got to know it and you got too want it.
And you got to *take* it.
          Reunion David Mamet

Strong and Weak Forms

There are common, every day words in English that change in pronunciation depending on how they are used in conversation. They are short, simple words, generally prepositions, pronouns, conjunctions, and a few verbs that are pronounced one way when they are given strong stress and another way when they are given weak stress. These are called *Strong and Weak Forms*.

    Example: Did Paul find the *cat*?
          He found *a* cat.

	Strong Form	*Weak Form*
a	eĭ	ə
	a cat	a *cat*

The main words in English that have strong and weak forms are: *a, am, an, and, are, as, at, be, been, but, can, could, do, does, for, from, had, has, have, he, her, him, his, just, me, must, of, shall, she, should, some, than, that, the, them, there, to, us, was, we, were, who, would, you.*

Practice saying the following words using both Strong and Weak Forms:

are

ɑə   John and Mary *are* going.

ɚ   John and *Mary* are going.

as

æz   *As* I was saying.

əz   As I was *saying.*

at

æt   He's *at* the theater.

ət   He's at the *theater.*

be

biː   Where will you *be* at 4:00?

bi   Where will you be at *4:00?*

but

bʊt   That's fine, *but* it's too late.

bət   That's fine, but it's too *late.*

can

kæn   *Can* I go?

kən   Can I *go?*

could

kʊd   She *could* play the part.

kəd   Do *you* think she could play the part?

do

duː   I'll *do* it!

du, də   *I'll* do it!

does

dʌz   What *does* he do all day?

dəz   What does he *do* all day?

for

fɔɚ   Which candidate are you *for?*

fɔ   *Which* candidate are you for?

from

frʌm   Are you *from* Tennessee?

frəm   No, I'm from *Alabama*.

had

hæd   He *had* a red car.

həd   No, he had a *green* car.

has

hæs   She *has* to go.

həs   She has to *stay*.

have

hæv   Do you *have* to go?

həv   I have to *go*.

of

ʌv   He's *of* the theater.

əv   She's of the *best* family.

or

ɔɚ   You can stay *or* you can leave.

ɔ   You can *come* or *go*.

to

tu   She's going *to* the park.

tə   She's going to the *park*.

that

ðæt   *That's* the one I want.

ðət   That's the one *I* want.

was

wɒz   Don *was* the other man in the room.

wəz   *Don* was the other man in the room.

would

wʊd   *Would* you ask her out?

wəd   Would *you* ask her out?

Chapter XI
The Singing Voice

The singing voice is an area that is frequently neglected when training the actor's speaking voice, which is surprising since actors who can sing well are in great demand. One of the principal reasons for this neglect is that training for the singing voice is generally separated from training for the speaking voice. In most universities, singing is taught in the music department and speaking in the theater department. The two only meet in the productions of musicals.

In teaching voice and speech to young theater students, I often find that at the start of their training I hear thin, reedy unsupported voices speaking in a high pitch that trails off into vocal fry at the ends of phrases. Many of these students tell me that they have been studying singing for several years. Why, I keep asking myself (and them), can't they apply the same principles of support and placement taught in singing to their speaking voices? They seem to have two voices: one for singing and one for speaking, and they don't always go together.

That's when I began to explore with them what they were doing in their singing training that was different from speaking and their answers were very interesting.

First, they told me that their singing teachers seldom, if ever, mentioned the speaking voice. If they did it was to caution them against using it in such a way that would adversely affect their singing voices. The problem was they didn't tell them how to do that.

Some of their singing teachers came exclusively from an operatic or choral music background, some from the musical theater. The operatic teachers often tended to caution their students about involvement in musical theater because musicals involved particular techniques such as "belting," which they thought might adversely affect their operatic voice. The musical theater teachers, on the other hand, often warned that singing techniques from the world of opera would give them a classical sound that could undermine what they were trying to achieve in their training for singing in musical theater. While musical theater voice teachers were generally more understanding of the need for good vocal technique for the speaking voice in musicals, they didn't know how to help the students achieve it. Some students were even told by their singing teachers to "save" their singing voices from the effects of vocal fry by only using the head voice when speaking, which produced thin reedy high-pitched tones. Some students were even told to limit speaking altogether to "save" their singing voice.

Since writing the first edition of this book, I have done a good deal of work with some of finest opera companies in the United States such as the Metropolitan Opera, The Lyric Opera of Chicago, and Chicago Opera Theater, working with opera singers on both their speaking voices and applying some of the techniques of the theater to their singing voices, such as dialects and diction. I found that opera singers were far more open and responsive to the demands of the speaking voice and entertained very few of the prejudices I found in the singing teachers at universities.

The following areas need to be more fully explored by singer/actors to make sure that their singing and speaking techniques are functioning as one.

Breathing

The techniques for breathing in the speaking and the singing voice are often at odds, confusing the student, who then fails to establish firm breath support for either the singing or the speaking voice. For instance, the quick inhalation or catch breath required by the actor in speaking quickly in coordination with the phrasing of the text may be difficult for the singer trained to breathe with the carefully coordinated demands of phrasing of the music. In reality the breath fuels the thought and the emotion in both singing and speaking. The breath support is the same, only more sustained in singing.

Example: Singing Voice

Frankie and Johnny

Frankie and Johnny were lovers, (breath)
Oh Lordy, how they could love, (breath)
They swore to be true to each other, (breath)

> Just as true as the stars above; (breath)
> He was her man, (breath)
> But he done her wrong. (breath)

Example: Speaking Voice

> *Coriolanus* by William Shakespeare (Volumnia)
> "I pray you daughter sing; (breath) or express yourself in a more comfortable sort. (breath) If my son were my husband, I should freelier rejoice in that absence wherein he won honour than in the embracements of his bed where he would show most love. (breath)

> *The Price* by Arthur Miller (Esther)
> "What do you mean a few dollars? (breath) I want to understand what you're saying! (breath) You knew he had money left? (breath)
> It's a farce. (breath) It's a goddamned farce! (breath)

For both the singing and the speaking voice, the breath supports the thought and the feeling being expressed.

Placement

The placement of the voice for singing is often confused with the placement of the voice for speaking, producing overdeveloped head tones in the speaking voice and little or no chest resonance. It is necessary to find an optimal pitch for the speaking voice that blends in chest resonance. Too many singers only use the head voice when speaking, which makes them sound thin and high-pitched. The lower pitch of the speaking voice doesn't mean that a singer can't move up into the falsetto range for the high notes and then come down again to the middle range when speaking.

Pitch

There needs to be less confusion about pitch between the singing and the speaking voice. Just because a singer is a tenor or a soprano, doesn't mean that the speaking voice must be high as well.

There is also confusion about the terms "head voice" and "chest voice." The "head voice" or the falsetto register in singing isn't generally used in the speaking voice. But the term can be confusing and could cause an actor who is used to singing terminology to use only head tones when speaking.

The speaking voice only uses what is called the "chest voice" in singing terms. However, this doesn't mean that the speaking voice is pushed down in the chest; indeed the placement of the voice in the resonators of the frontal bones of the face is the same. It's just a question of confusion caused by terminology.

Resonance

Resonance for the speaking voice must be balanced on optimal pitch between the head resonator and the chest resonator. I sometimes hear actor/singers, especially women, who have a tense nasal sound in their speaking voice because they are used to tensing the soft palate for belting. In speaking only the three nasal consonants **m n ŋ** come through the nose, the other sounds are released through the mouth. This means that the soft palate must be flexible. Practice the exercises for nasality and denasality, switching between the nasal consonants and the vowels to strengthen the soft palate.

Articulation

Singers, as well as actors, need to articulate and develop clarity of diction as well as dexterity in their use of articulated language. Opera singers frequently sing in so many languages that they forget that the words and their meaning are just as important as their beautiful sound. Actors, on the other, hand, may not articulate with the same precision when they sing as when they speak.

Text

Singers need to find a way to speak the text without declaiming and to develop the ability to communicate meaning clearly and simply. Reading aloud using poetry and heightened text such as Shakespeare's Sonnets or speeches can be very helpful for singers as well as actors. It is also helpful for singers to speak the lyrics of a song before they begin to work on the music, to get a sense of what the words mean, how they relate to the meaning of song, and how the song fits into the story being told in the musical.

Flexibility in Terms of Approach

Opera singers should work on a variety of material, as should musical theater performers. Dawn Upshaw is a good example of an opera singer who can sing musical theater material as brilliantly as she sings "Bati Bati" from *Don Giovanni*.

Control of Emotional Involvement in Performance

The singer needs to be able to control emotional response to the material in performance that might affect the quality of the singing in the upper register while at the same time not letting voice production become mechanical. The actor must also not become so emotionally affected that the audience can't understand what is being said. It is important to remember that communicating thoughts and feelings through words and music to an audience involves a complex emotional response. There are no absolute rules, and there must be balance.

I hope for the day when theater training institutions will implement joint training of both the speaking and the singing voice with full communication between teachers of singing and speaking. Teachers, students, and audiences will all benefit.